Learning Chess - Chess for Beginners

I dedicate this book to my parents. Your love is the greatest gift on this earth.

Thank you for everything, yours Alexander.

Learning Chess - Chess for Beginners

by Alexander Fischer
Translator: Dana Comstock

Bibliographic Information of the German National Library
The German National Library lists this publication in the German National Bibliography; detailed bibliographic data can be found online at http://dnb.dnb.de.

ISBN   9783755730057

Production and publishing:BoD – Books on Demand, Norderstedt

Copyright   © 2022 Alexander Fischer, 1. Auflage

Translator: Dana Comstock

Homepage   www.schach-lernen.de
                                  forum.schach-lernen.de
                                  blog.schach-lernen.de
                                  shop.schach-lernen.de

Table of Contents

Table of Contents

Learning Chess – Chess for Beginners

If you want to learn chess as a beginner, I want to teach you the basics of playing chess and the rules of chess in this book "Learning Chess – Chess for Beginners" in a comprehensive way.

Many believe that it's hard to learn chess. But if you learn the few rules that there are, you'll see that it's not that hard. Chess isn't so hard to learn after all. This book aims to encourage you to start playing chess. Once you have finished this book, you will have mastered the rules of chess.

All examples are clearly and comprehensively structured using graphics. Each move of a chess piece is shown in a diagram. With this guide, you'll comprehensively learn chess.

Chess is a Sport

Chess is very demanding for players. Playing chess fosters skills like concentration, self-discipline, perseverance and mathematical thinking. It's also very competitive, since you can train in playing chess and improve that way.

"Chess is stimulation and pleasure at the same time. It educates the young and invigorates the old. The sport of chess promotes skills such as concentration, the ability to observe and comprehend, combination and perseverance, skills that are generally useful in life" (Former Federal President Richard von Weizsäcker)

I'm convinced that with this book, starting to play chess will be easy for you and I hope you will enjoy learning the game of chess, which is also called "the game of kings".

To be able to understand the rules better, you should set up a chess board, so that the examples involving many comprehensive diagrams will be even easier to understand.

The Chessboard

Chess is a strategic board game. It is played by two opponents, on a so-called chessboard, which has a square shape with even more squares on it. On each side there are eight squares. So since it is 8 x 8, there are 64 squares. Those are alternately white (light) and black (dark).

The Chessboard - Designation of the Individual Squares

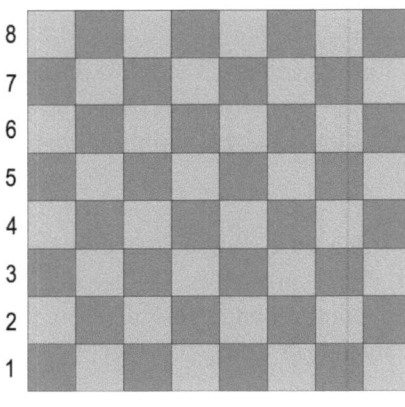

There are letters and numbers at the edges of the chessboard. On the left side, there are numbers next to the eight squares. Those are numbered from 1 to 8.

On the bottom side, there are letters under the eight squares. They are labeled from a to h.

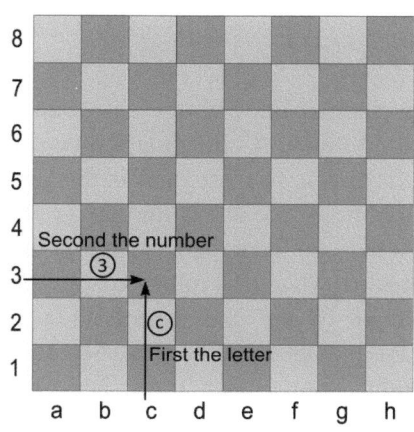

To indicate the squares on the chessboard, you use the letter that is under the square first, then the number that is on the left of that square. So it is always the letter first, then the number.

This way, there is only one square where there is a "c", for example, on the letter-side and, for example, a "3" on the number-side. This would be the square c3. This way, each square has its own unique designation.

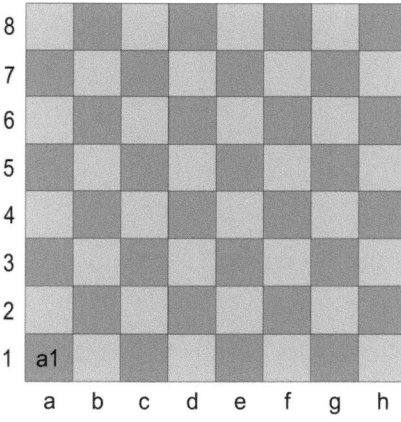

Example:
The square on the bottom left is indicated as a1.

	a	b	c	d	e	f	g	h
8	a8	b8	c8	d8	e8	f8	g8	h8
7	a7	b7	c7	d7	e7	f7	g7	h7
6	a6	b6	c6	d6	e6	f6	g6	h6
5	a5	b5	c5	d5	e5	f5	g5	h5
4	a4	b4	c4	d4	e4	f4	g4	h4
3	a3	b3	c3	d3	e3	f3	g3	h3
2	a2	b2	c2	d2	e2	f2	g2	h2
1	a1	b1	c1	d1	e1	f1	g1	h1

Each square and its designation. This is important for the notation of moves. More on this later.

The Chessboard – The Ranks, Files, Diagonals and their Designations

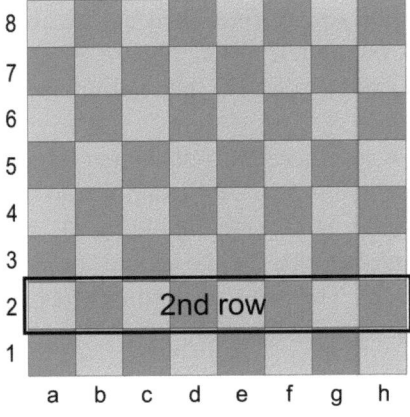

The horizontal lines on the chessboard are called ranks. A chessboard consists of eight ranks. The 1st rank is the one on the bottom, the 8th is the one at the top. So they go from the left edge of the chessboard, where the number is, to the right edge of the chessboard, viewed from the player at the bottom. So there are eight squares each time. This, for example, is the 2nd rank (a2 – h2).

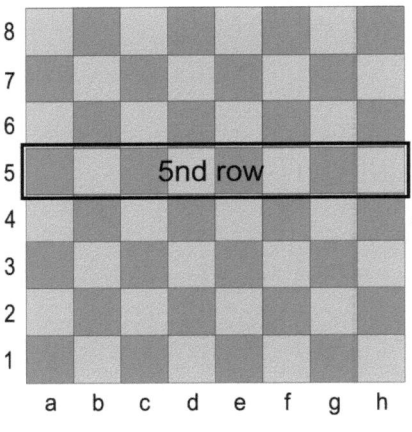

This is the 5th rank (a5 – h5).

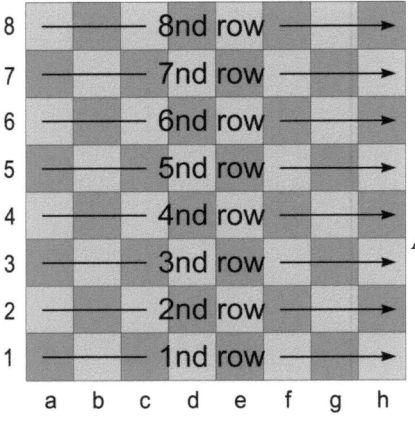

All ranks and their designation.

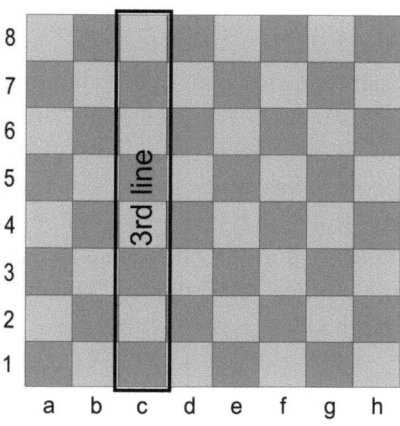

The vertical lines on the chessboard are called files. Just like the ranks, there are eight files on a chessboard. The 1st file is the one on the far left, the 8th is the one on the far right. So they go from the bottom edge of the chessboard to the top edge, viewed from the player at the bottom.

So there are eight squares each time. This, for example, is the 3rd file (c1 – c8).

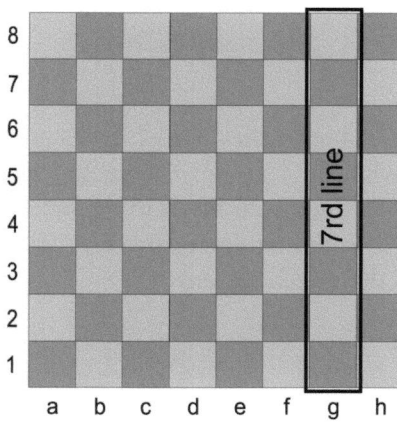

This, for example, is the 7th file (g1 – g8).

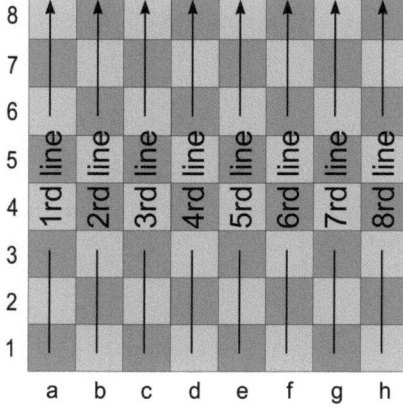

All files and their designation.

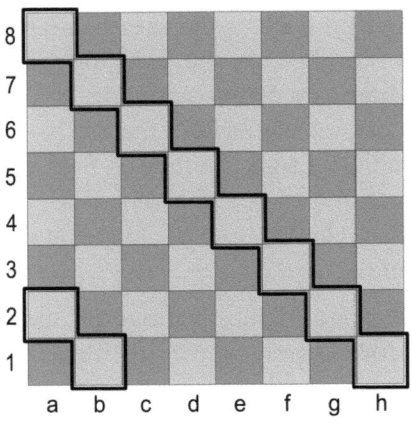

A chessboard also consists of diagonal (angled) squares. The diagonals are a continuous sequence of squares of the same color. So either white or black squares, from one side of the edge of the chessboard to the other. The longest diagonal on a chessboard is eight squares, the shortest is two squares.

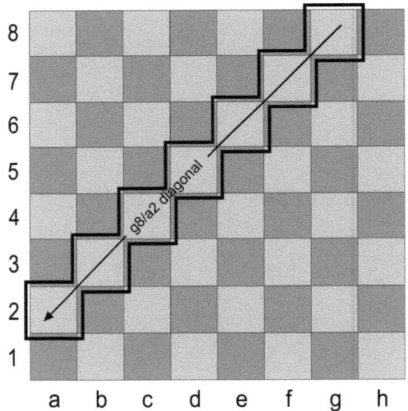

In this example, they are white squares. And what do you call a diagonal like this? The line from the starting square, e.g. g8, to the target square, e.g. a2, is called the g8/a2 diagonal.

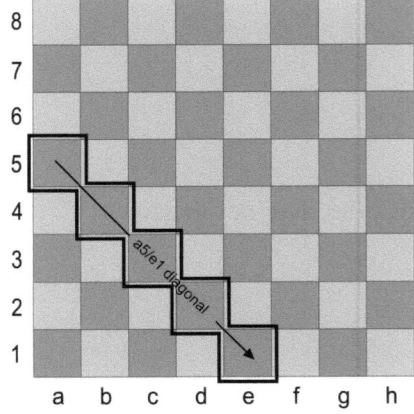

Here we see the black squares. The starting square is a5. This diagonal is called a5/e1.

Setting up the Chessboard Correctly

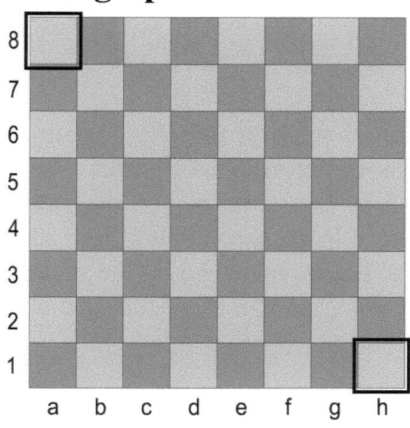

The chessboard is set up so that there is a white square on the lower right-hand corner on the player side, so at the top or bottom edge of the chessboard. The squares h1 and a8 are always white.

If there happens to be a black square on the lower right, the chessboard is in the wrong position.

The Chess Pieces

There are 32 pieces in total. Each player has 16 pieces. One uses white and other uses black pieces. Among them are 6 different types of pieces in different quantities.

There are the following types of pieces:
Pawn, rook, knight, bishop, queen and king.

There are the following number of individual pieces:

	Black	White	
8 pawns			8 pawns
2 rooks			2 rooks
2 knights			2 knights
2 bishops			2 bishops
1 queen			1 queen
1 king			1 king

The Initial Setup

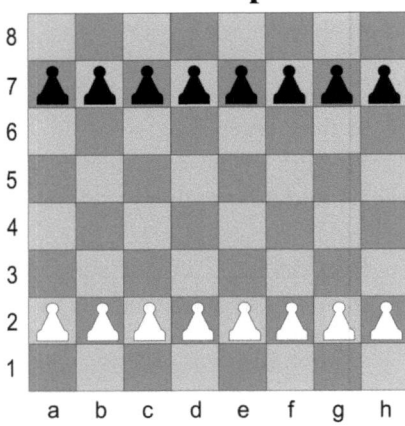

The initial setup of the chess pieces is the same before each game. When viewed by the white player, the pawns are placed in the second rank from a2 to h2. The black pawns are on the seventh rank from a7 to h7.

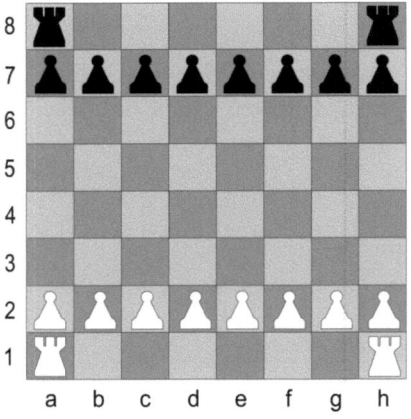

The first and eighth rank for the player at the bottom are called the back ranks.

On the left and right edges in the first rank, that is, on a1 and h1, are the white rooks (tower shape), and on the eighth rank, a8 and h8, are the black rooks.

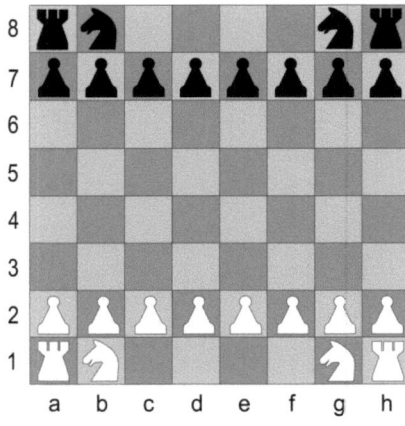

The white knights (horse head shape) are placed on the squares b1 and g1 and the black knights on b8 and g8 at the start of the game.

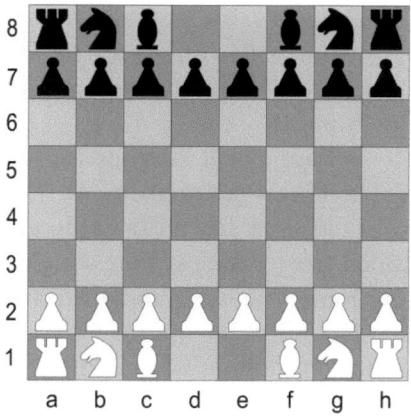

Each player has two bishops. They are on the squares c1 (black square) and f1 (white square), as well as c8 (white square) and f8 (black square). This way, each player has a bishop to move across the white squares and one to move across the black squares.

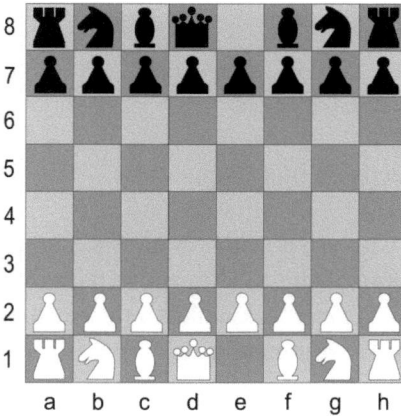

The white queen is on square d1 of the player's color – on a white square, and the black queen is placed on d8 of the player's color – a black square.

There is a rule for queens: "White queens on white squares, black queens on black squares."

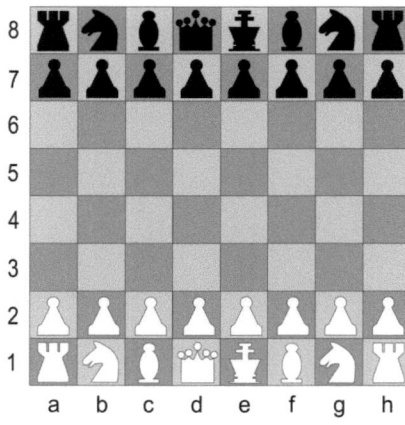

The white king (the king is the tallest piece) is placed on the last empty square in the first rank, e1, and the black king is placed on the square e8 in the eighth rank.

This is the initial setup.

Queenside and Kingside

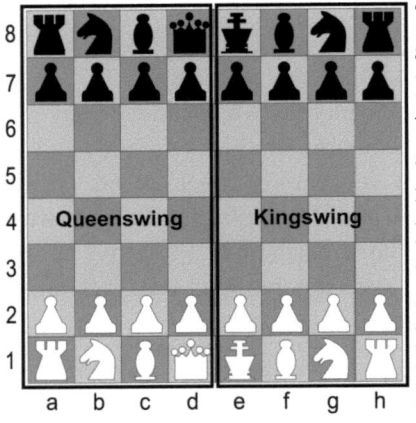

The files from a1 – a8, b1 – b8, c1 – c8 and d1 – d8 are called queenside (to the left of the queen's initial position) and the files from e1 – e8, f1- f8, g1 – g8 and h1 – h8 are called kingside (to the right of the king's initial position). The pieces on the right side of the king are also called king bishops, king knights and king rook. The same applies to the pieces to the left of the queen. They are called queen bishops, queen knights and queen rook.

Remember:

The pieces have to be exactly opposite from each other.

White queens on white squares, black queens on black squares.

A draw is made beforehand to determine who starts with white. The player using the white pieces always opens the game of chess. They move the piece from the starting square to the target square. Then black makes a move, then white again, so that both players always move alternately.

It is always compulsory to move, skipping a move not allowed. However, there is no obligation to capture.

The King

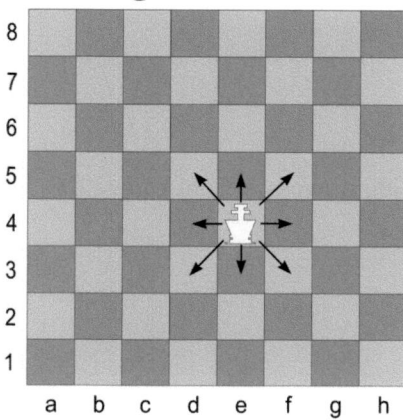

The king is only allowed to move one square, but it can go in any direction, horizontally, vertically or diagonally. The king cannot jump over other pieces.

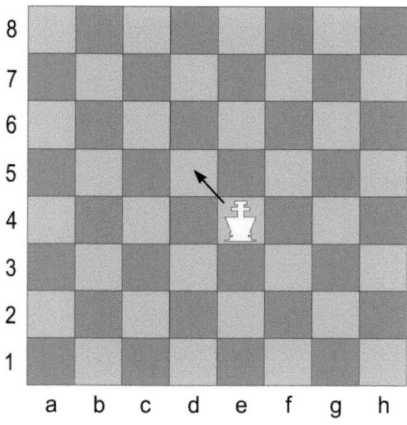

The king moves from square e4 ..

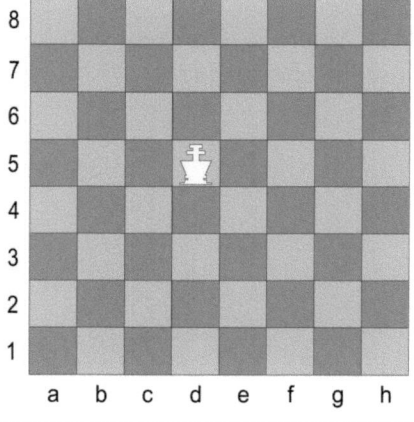

.. to square d5.

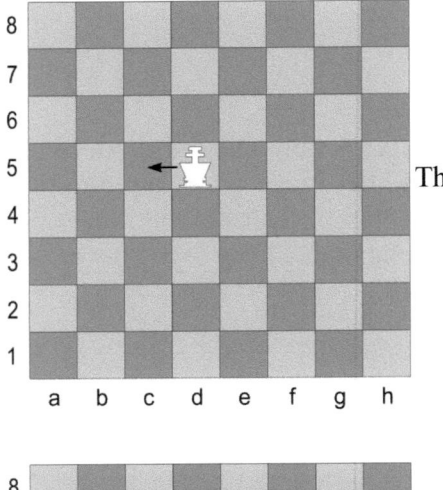

The king moves on from square d5 ..

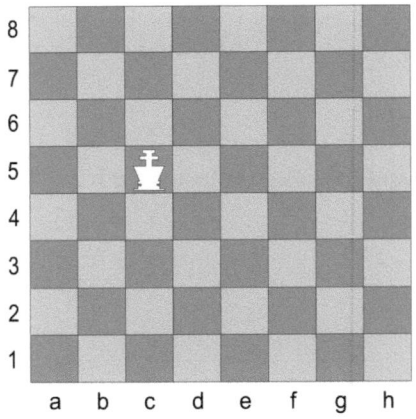

... to square c5.

Remember:
The king is the most important piece in chess. You have to prevent your king from being checkmated. Otherwise you lose the chess game.

The Queen

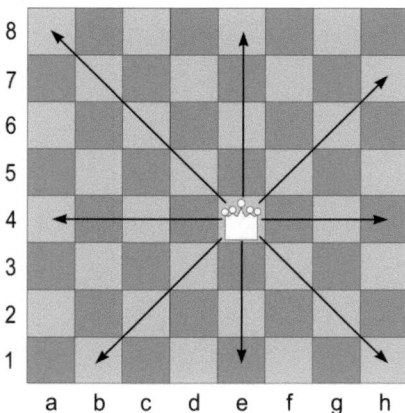

The Queen is a major piece. In the initial setup, the white queen is on square d1 and the black queen is on square d8.

The queen can move in any direction – horizontally, vertically or diagonally. It can move several squares at a time and can go to any desired square. It can reach any square on the chessboard. The queen cannot jump over any pieces.

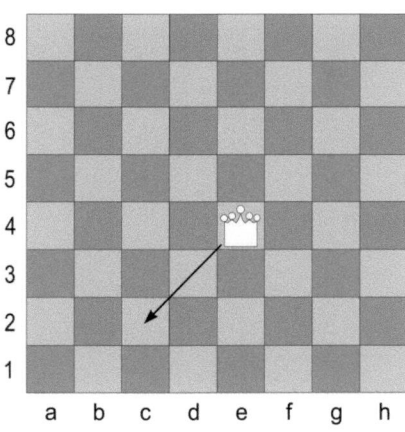

The queen moves from square e4 ..

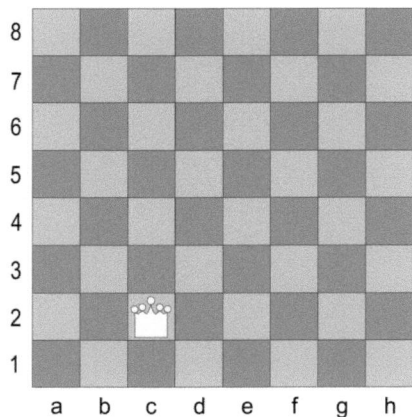

.. to square c2.

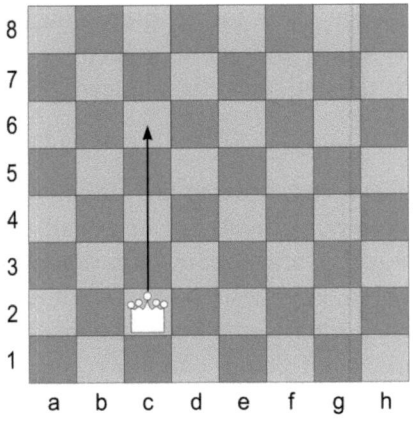

The queen moves on from square c2 ..

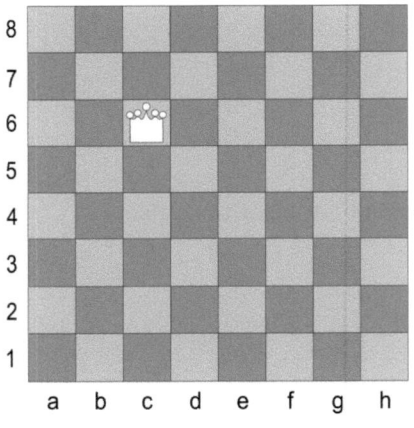

.. to square c6.

Remember:
The queen is the strongest piece with the most possible moves.

The Rook

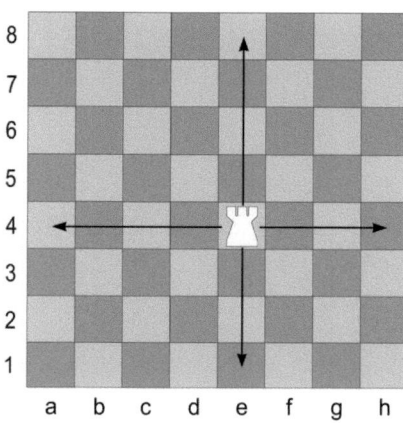

In the initial setup, the rooks are at the corners, the white ones on a1 and h1, the black ones on a8 and h8. The rook is also a major piece.

The rook moves horizontally on the ranks and vertically on the files. It is also allowed to move backwards. This way, it can move several squares at a time and go to any square. It can reach all squares of the chessboard. The rook cannot jump over other pieces.

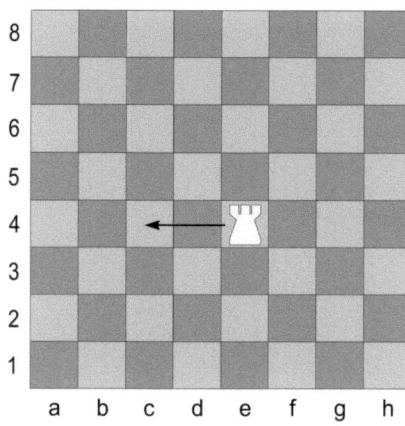

Here, the rook moves horizontally from square e4 ..

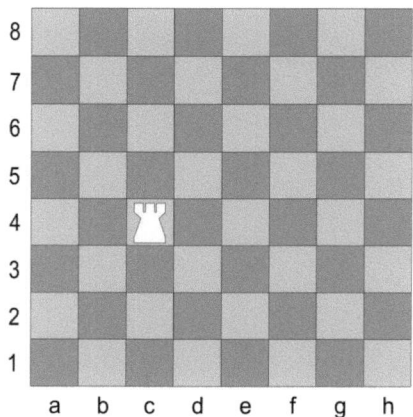

.. to square c4.

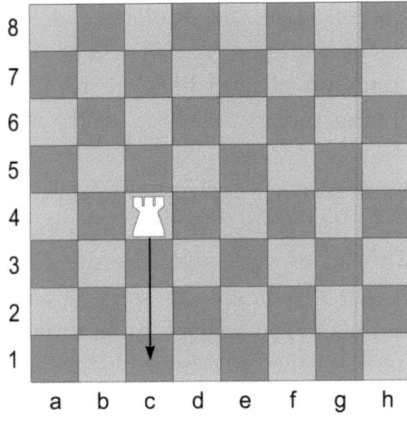

The rook moves on vertically from square c4 ..

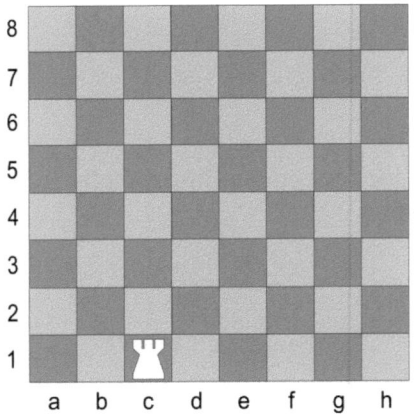

.. to square c1.

Remember:
The rook dominates the vertical and horizontal squares.

The Bishop

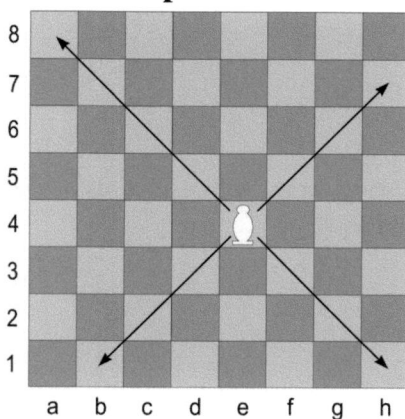

The bishop is a minor piece. In the initial setup, the white bishops are on the squares c1 and f1, the black bishops are on the squares c8 and f8. The bishop can only move diagonally. It can move forwards and backwards across the same diagonal. It can move several squares at a time and can go to any square. The bishop cannot jump over other pieces.

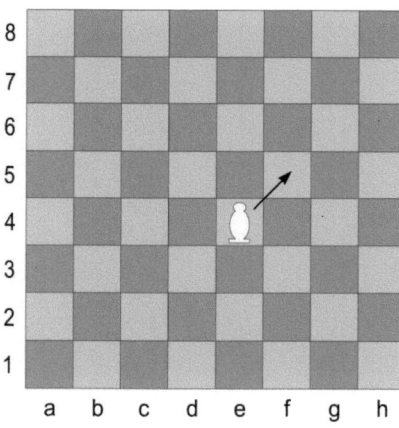

A bishop on a white square can only move across white squares.

The bishop on the white squares moves from square e4 ..

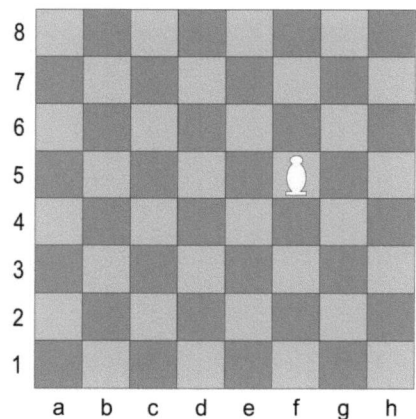

.. to square f5.

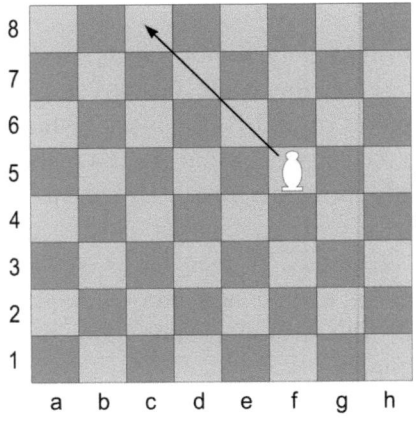

The bishop on the white squares moves on from square f5 ..

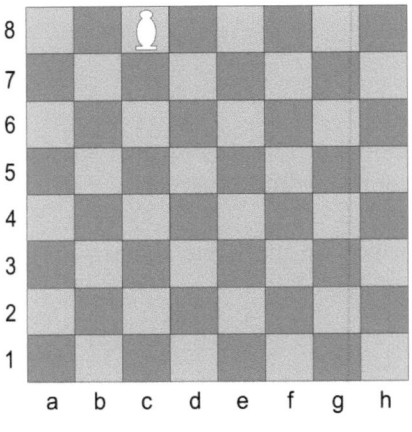

.. to square c8.

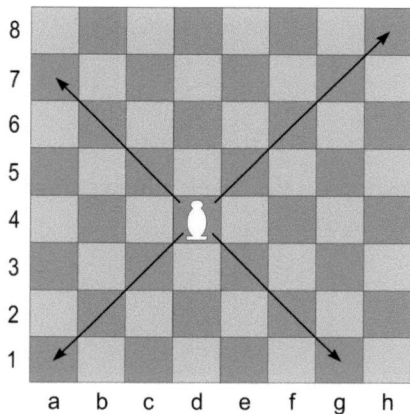

A bishop on a black square can only move across black squares.

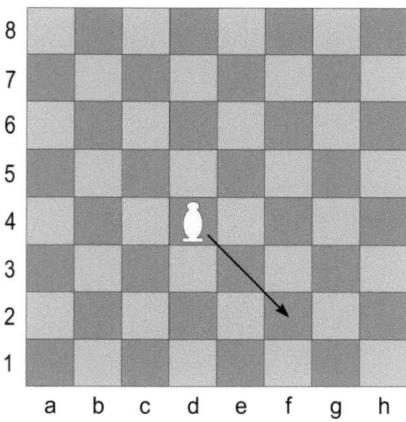

The bishop on the black squares moves from square d4 ..

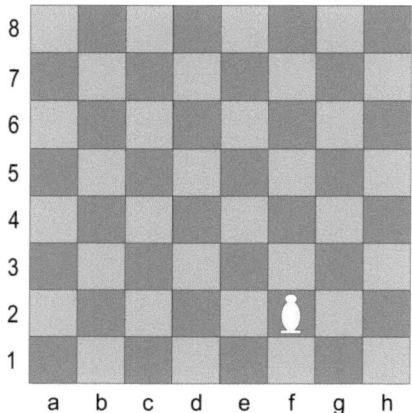

.. to square f2.

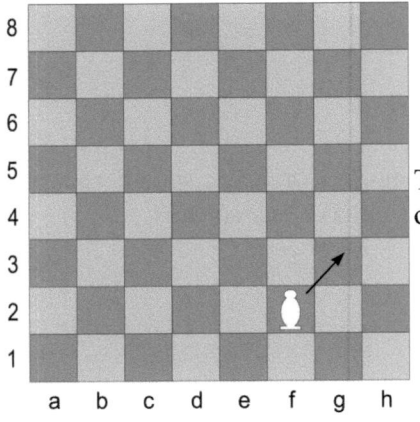

The bishop on the black squares moves on from square f2 ..

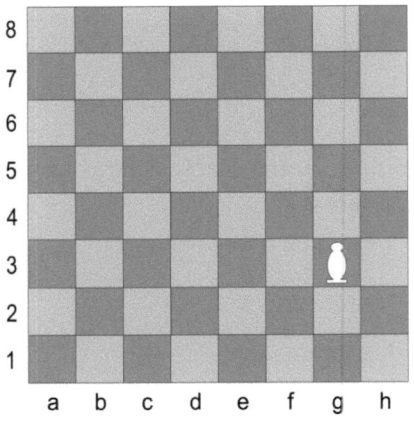

.. to square g3.

Remember:
Bishops cannot change their square color and have to stay on the diagonal squares of the same color.

The Knight

The knight is a minor piece like the bishop. In the initial setup, the knights are on the squares b1 and g1 (white) and b8 and g8 (black).

The special feature of the knight is that it is the only chess piece that can move (jump) over both your own and opposing pieces.

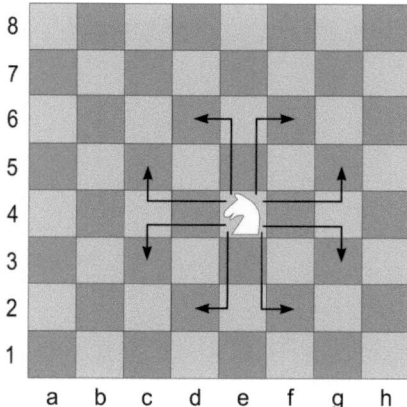

The knight moves two squares horizontally and then one square vertically. It can also move two squares vertically and then one square horizontally.

After each move, the square color changes. If the knight was on a white square, it will be on a black one after a move. Conversely, it moves from a black square to a white square.

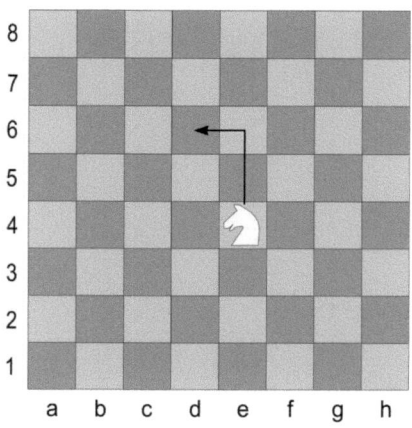

The knight moves from square e4 ..

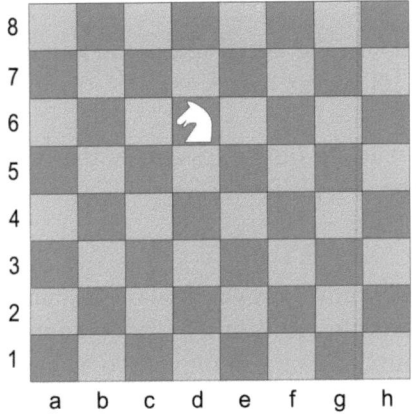

.. to square d6.

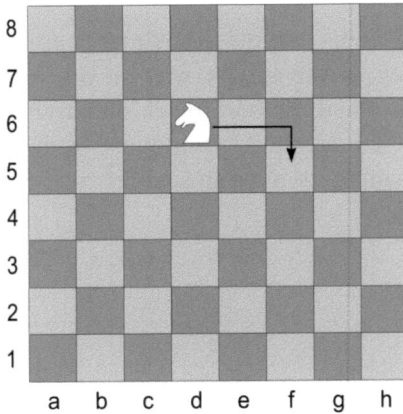

The knight moves on from square d6 ..

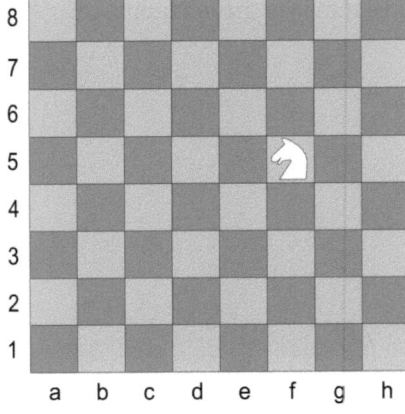

.. to square f5.

Remember:
The knight moves two squares in one direction, and then one square to the side (a so-called knight's move).
This move looks like an L.

The Pawn

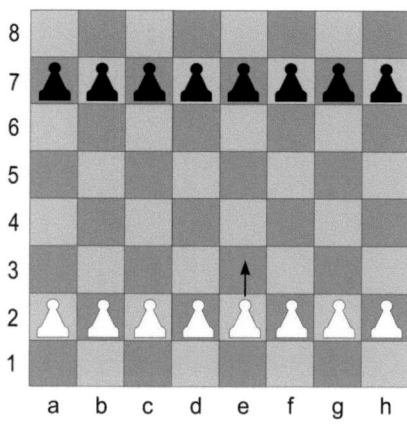

At the start, each player has eight pawns.

Unlike the other pieces, the pawn cannot move backwards, but only forwards.

The pawn can only move forward one square per move.

The pawn moves from square e2 ...

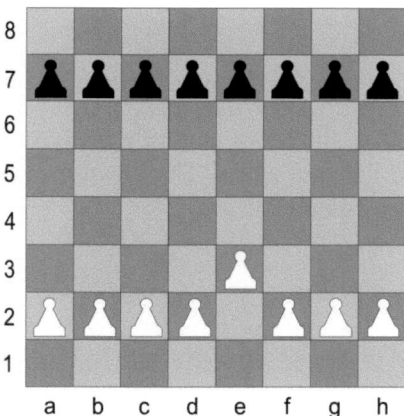

.. one square forward to e3.

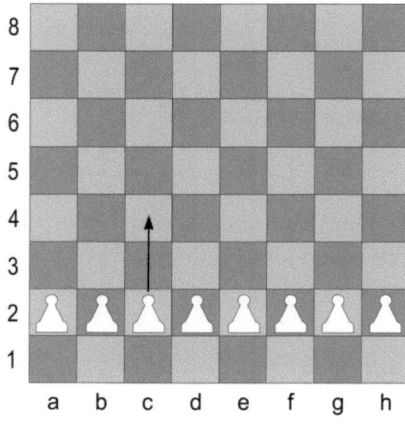

Exception: If the pawn has not yet been moved and is therefore still in the initial position (starting square, white a2 – h2, black a7 – h7), it can also move two squares forward, provided that the square in front of it and the target square are not occupied.

The pawn moves from the initial position on square c2 ..

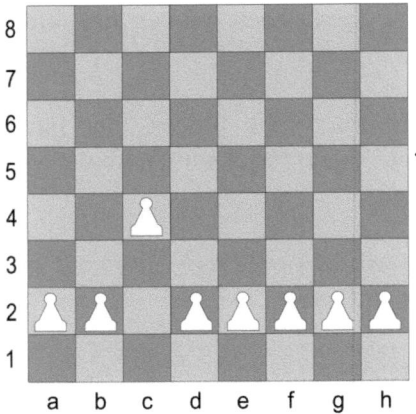

.. two squares forward to square c4.

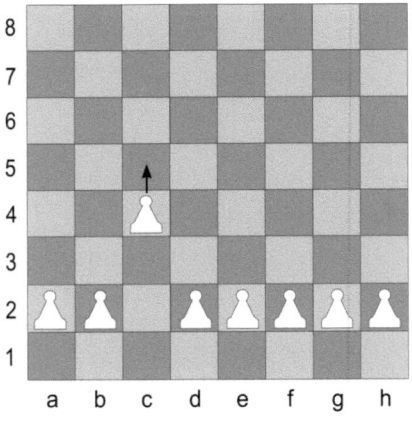

After that, the pawn can only move one square forward again. The pawn moves on from square c4 ..

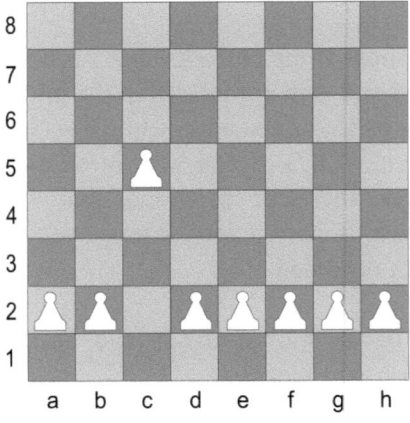

.. one square forward to c5.

This is what the chessboard looks like after the pawn's moves.

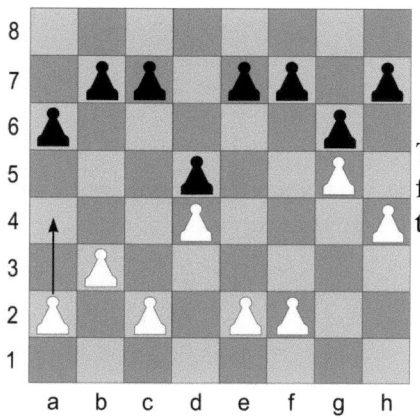

The pawn moves two squares forward from the initial position. From square a2 to square a4.

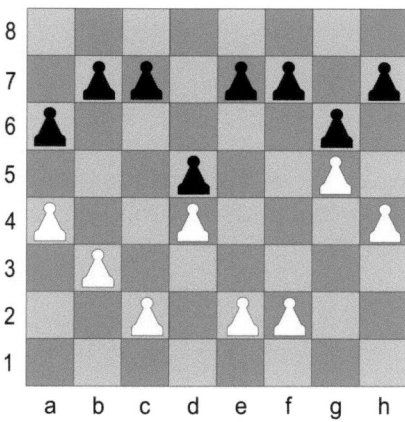

The pawn has moved to square a4.

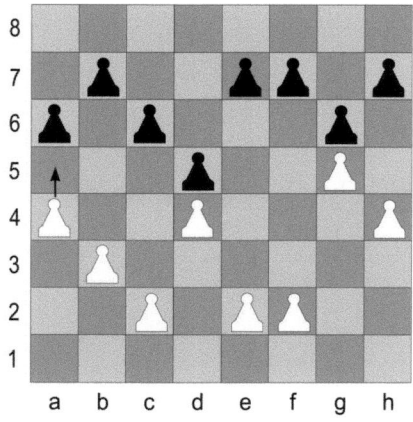

The pawn moves on from square a4 to square a5, after the opponent's turn (c7 to c6).

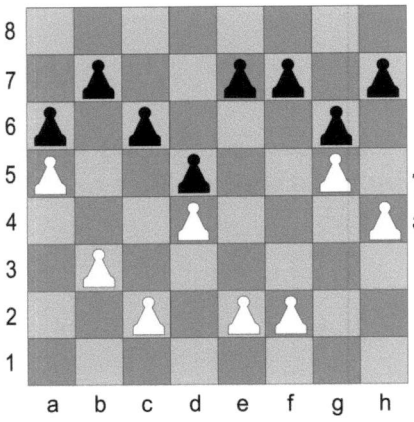

This is what the chessboard looks like after the pawn's moves.

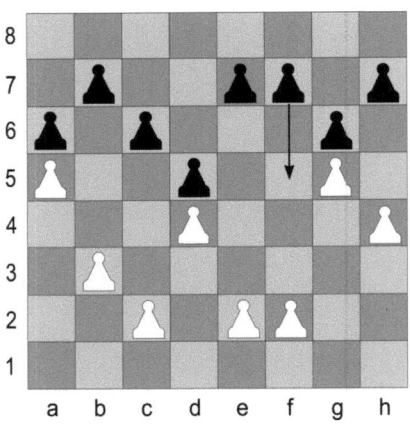

The pawn moves two squares forward from the initial position. From square f7 to square f5.

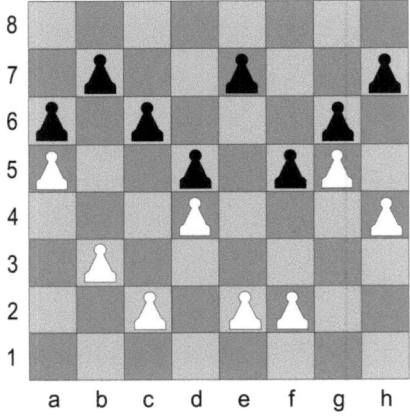

The pawn has moved to square f5.

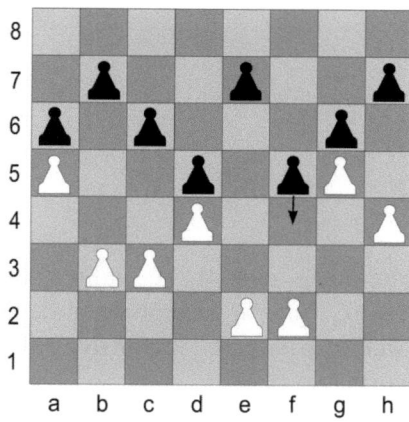

The pawn moves on from square f5 to square f4, after the opponent's turn (c2 to c3).

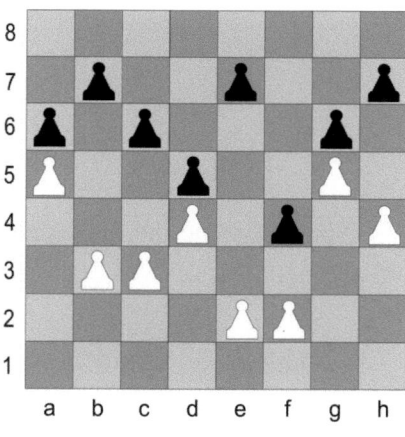

This is what the chessboard looks like after the pawn's moves.

Remember:
The pawn can only go one square forwards per move.

If the pawn is still in its initial position, it can move two squares forward. After that, it can only move one square forward.

The Value of the Pieces

The value of each piece in pawns:

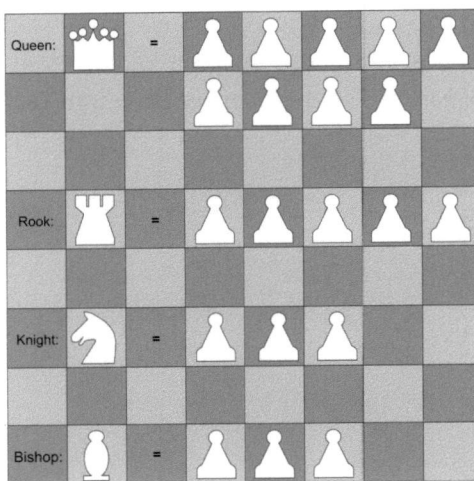

The king cannot be valued in pawns, since it cannot be traded. And a pawn is obviously only worth one pawn.

The value of the pieces among themselves. You can value the pieces not only with pawns, but also with other pieces.

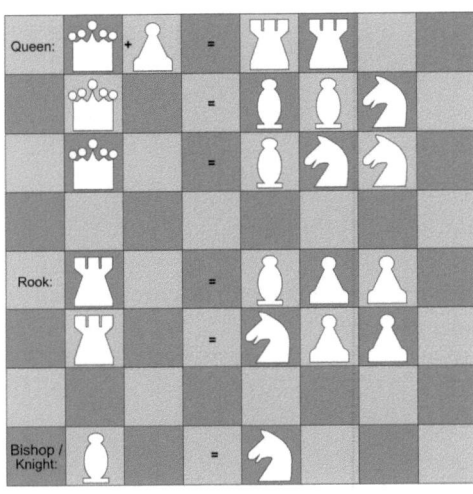

An example: If you lose your rook (worth 5 pawns) and take a knight (worth 3 pawns), you have lost two pawns. This means that the opponent would theoretically have two more pawns on the chessboard.

Capturing Pieces

Pieces of your own color, e.g. white, cannot be captured. There can only be one piece on each square. This way, your own and the opponent's pieces limit your range of motion.

If the square is occupied by your own piece, the move ends a square before it. Exception: The knight makes its move over your own piece. If this square is occupied by the opponent's piece, you can capture it and the opponent's piece will be removed from the board. Exception: The king cannot move to a square that is threatened by the opponent. However, there is no obligation to capture a piece.

The pieces cannot move as freely during a game of chess as they could on an empty chessboard.

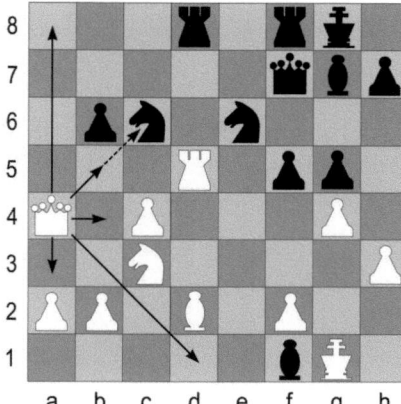

The white queen on square a4 can move horizontally to the square b4. The queen cannot go further, because your own pawn occupies the square c4. Vertically, the queen can move to the squares a5 – a8 and the square a3. Another pawn of your own color, square a2, hinders the queen from moving further. Diagonally, the queen can go to the squares b3, c2, d1 and b5. The queen could also take the black knight on square c6, however.

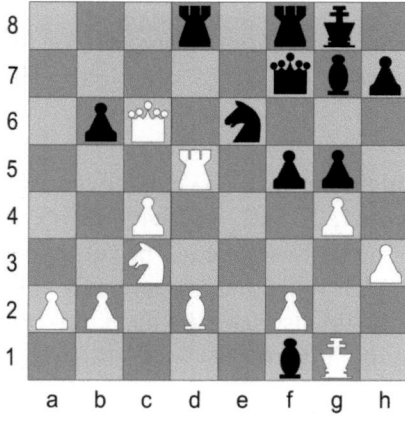

The white queen moves from square a4 to square c6 and takes the black knight.

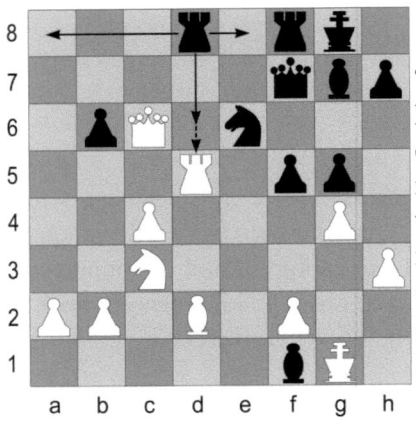

The black rook on square d8 can move horizontally to the squares c8 – a8 and e8. The rook cannot go further to the right, because your own rook occupies the square f8. Vertically, the rook can move to the squares d7 – d6. The rook could also take the white rook on square d5, however.

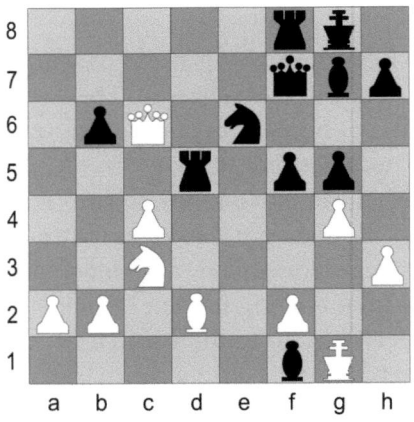

The black rook moves from square d8 to square d5 and takes the white rook.

Remember:

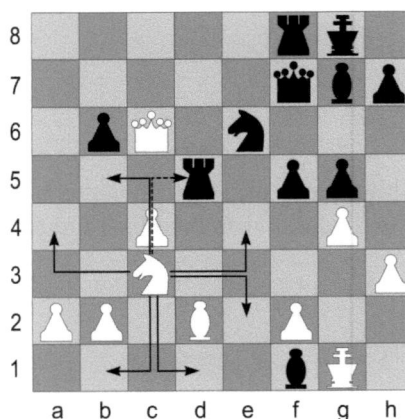

You cannot jump over your own or the opponent's pieces. Exception: The knight.

The knight on square c3 can move to the squares a4, b1, d1, e2, e4 and b5. It cannot move to square a2, because your own pawn occupies square a2. The knight could also take the black rook on square d5, however.

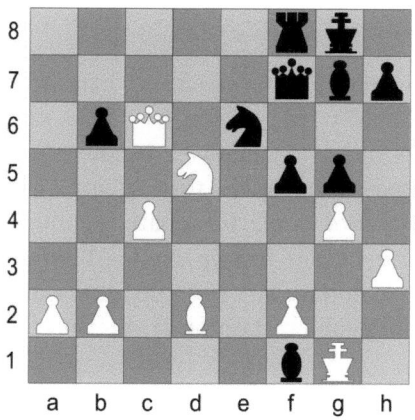

The knight moves from square c3 to square d5 (moves over your own pawn) and takes the black rook.

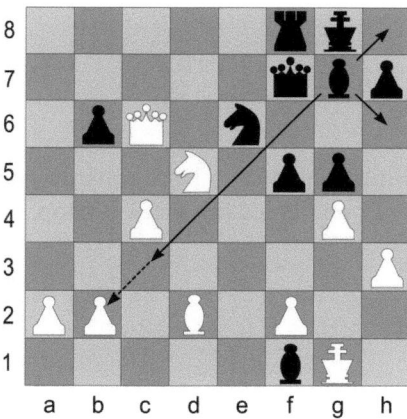

The black bishop on square g7 can move to the squares h6 and h8 diagonally. It cannot move to the square f8, because your own rook occupies that square. It can move further to the diagonal squares f6, e5, d4 and c3. The black bishop could also take the white pawn on square b2, however.

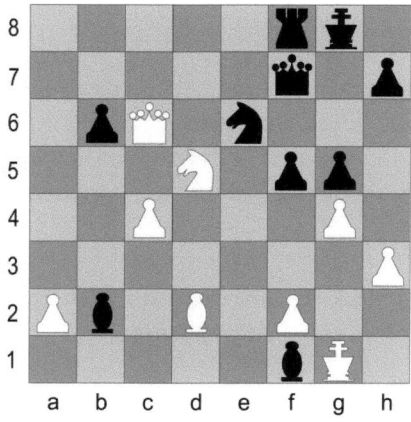

The black bishop moves from square g7 to square b2 and takes the white pawn.

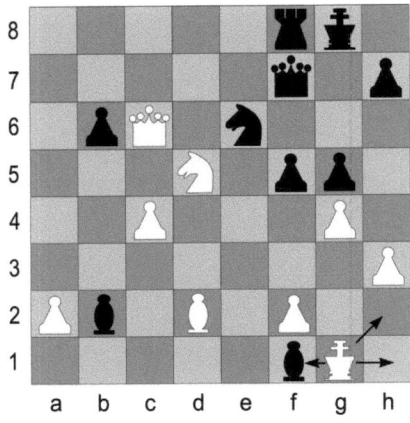

The white king on square g1 can move horizontally to square h1. The king cannot move to square f2, because your own pawn occupies that square. The king cannot move to square g2 either, because of the bishop on f1. It could move to square h2. The king could also take the black bishop on f1, however.

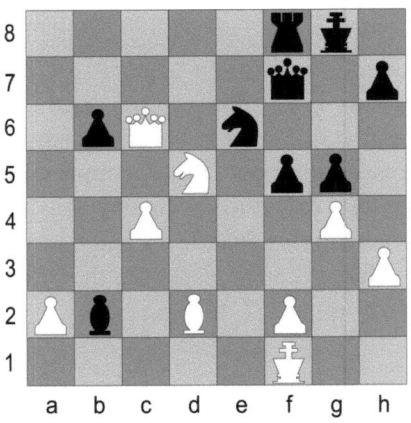

The white king moves from square g1 to square f1 and takes the black bishop.

Remember:

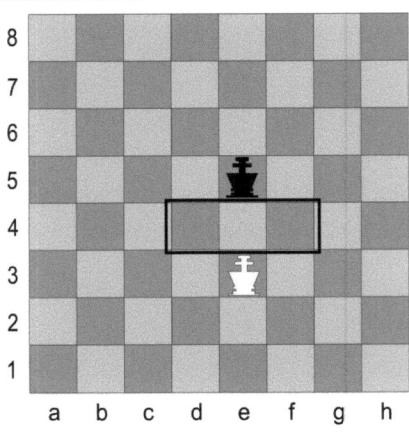

Between the two kings, there always has to be at least one square, since a king may not move to a threatened square, which is threatened by an opponent's piece.

When the kings are opposite from each other, this is called opposition.

Capturing Pieces using Pawns

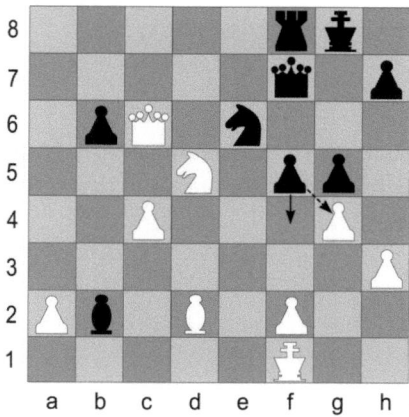

The pawn has a special rule for capturing. It can only take pieces that are diagonally in front of it on the squares to the left or right. The pawn is the only piece that captures other pieces in another direction than it moves in.

Vertically, the black pawn can move from square f5 to square f4. However, the black pawn could also take the white pawn on square g4.

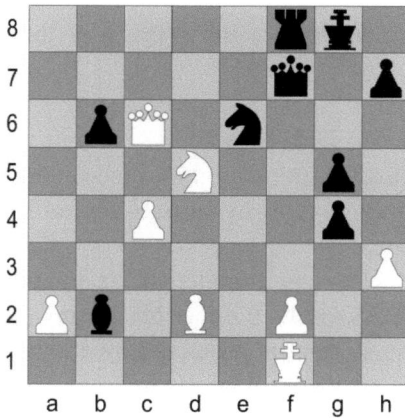

The black pawn moves diagonally from square f5 to square g4 and takes the white pawn.

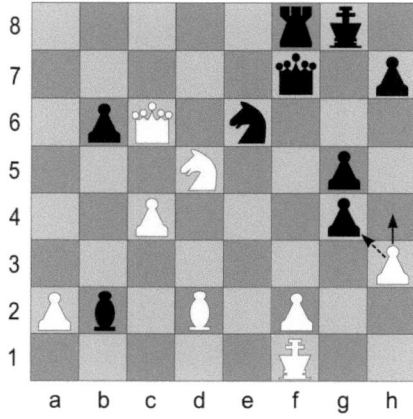

Vertically, the white pawn can move from square h3 to square h4. However, the white pawn could also take the black pawn on square g4.

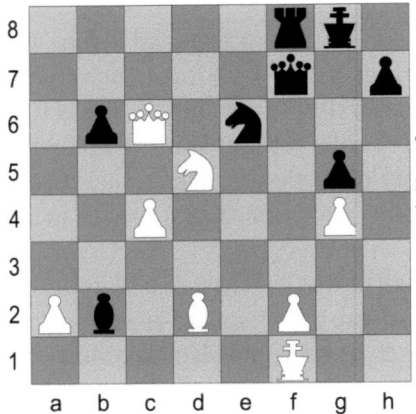

The black pawn moves diagonally from square h3 to square g4 and takes the black pawn.

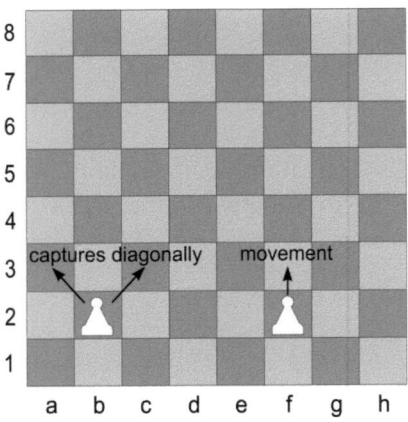

Remember:

Pieces can capture the same way they move.

Exception: The pawn.
The pawn captures other pieces only diagonally and always moves forward.

If the pawn is threatened, it cannot move backwards. It either has to stay on that square and be protected by another piece, or it can move forward.

Capturing En Passant (in Passing)

This is a special rule for pawns.

The black pawn that is still in its initial position (a7 – h7 for black, a2 – h2 for white) moves two squares (not a single square at a time) forward to a square next to the white pawn in the fifth rank, which attacks the square that the black pawn just passed (capturing direction). This way, it can take the black pawn like it only moved to the sixth rank, so one square forward. The white pawn moves to the square that the black pawn just moved over.

If you want to capture en passant, you have to do it right away in the following move. If the pawn is not taken, you cannot make this move later on.

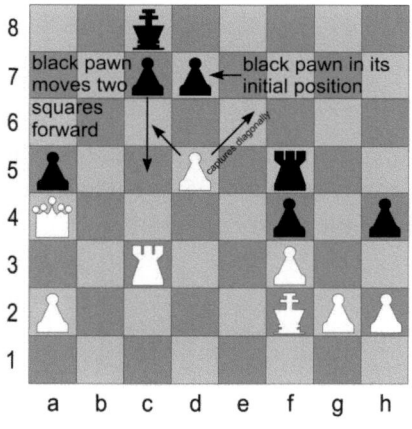

The black pawn moves two squares forward from its initial position on square c7 (seventh rank) ..

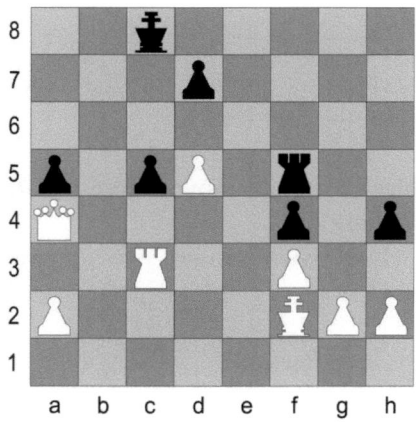

.. to the fifth rank, square c5, next to the white pawn.

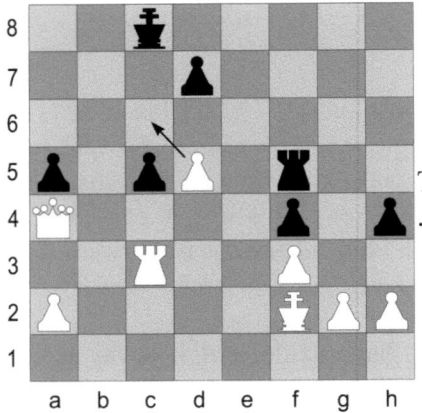

The white pawn moves from square d5 ..

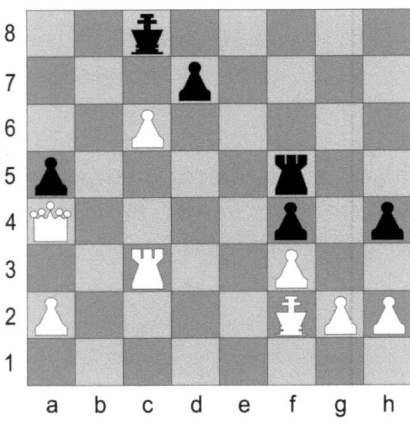

.. to square c6. This way, it can take the black pawn on square c5 like it had only moved to the sixth rank (square c6).

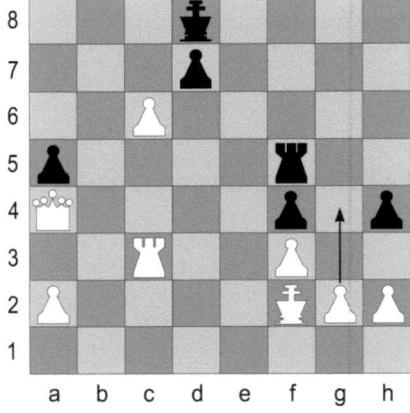

This rule also applies for the black pawns on the fourth rank.

The black king has moved from square c8 to square d8.
The white pawn moves two squares forward from its initial position on square g2 ..

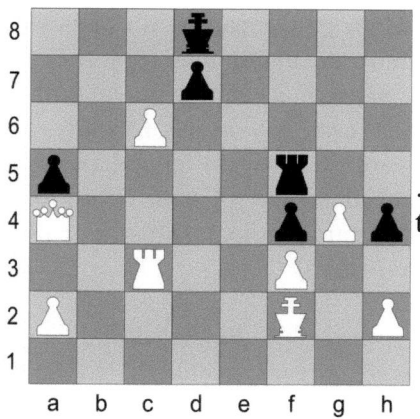

.. to the fourth rank, square g4, between the two black pawns.

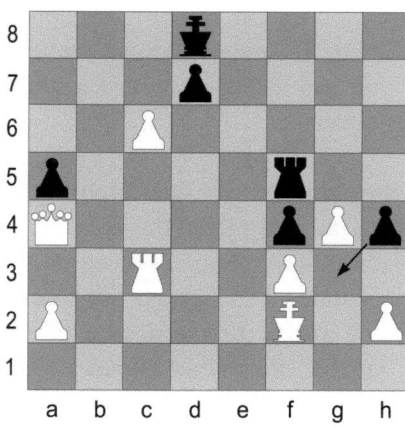

The black pawn moves from square h4 (the pawn on square f4 could also move instead) ..

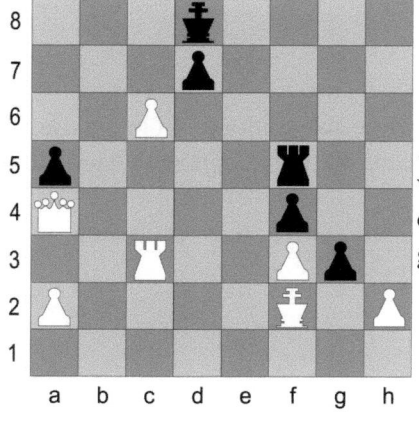

.. to square g3. This way, it can take the white pawn on square g4, like it had only moved to the third rank (square g3).

Promoting Pawns

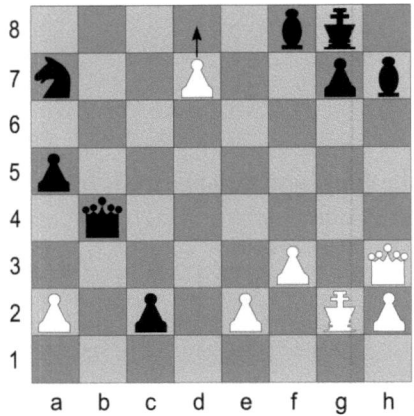

If a white pawn reaches the opposing back rank, the eighth rank (first rank for black pawns), it cannot move further. Since it can only move forward, not backward, it has to immediately be exchanged for any of your own pieces (of the same color). This is called promotion.

This promotion is limited to the pieces that were already captured. Normally, this is the queen, since it is the strongest piece. However, you can choose a rook, a bishop or a knight, the only exception is the king. If several pawns make it there, you can also play with e.g. three or four queens.

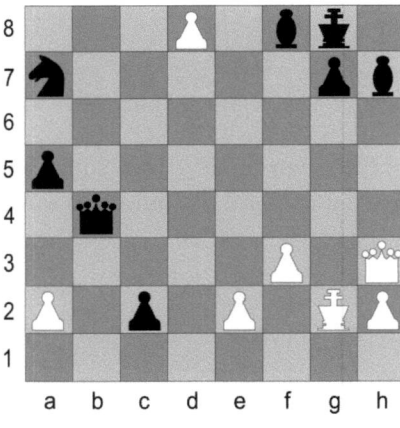

The promotion is completed by removing the pawn from the chessboard and placing the exchanged piece on the pawn's square. Right away, the piece's move and strike direction take effect. This means that the piece could immediately check or even mate.

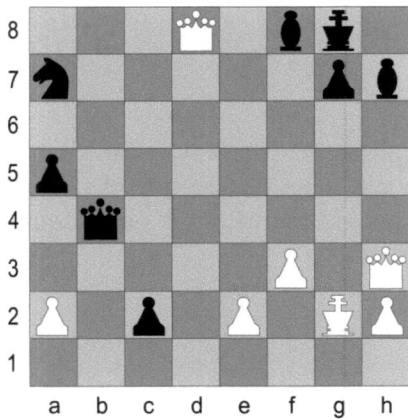

The white pawn moves from square d7 to square d8 on the opposing back rank.

Here, the pawn was promoted to a queen.

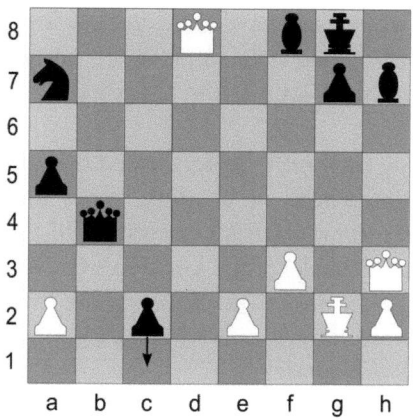

The black pawn moves to the back rank, from square c2 to square c1.

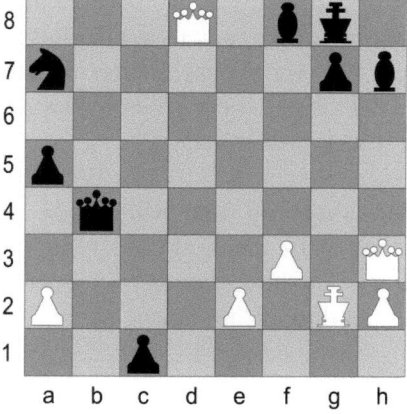

The black pawn has reached the back rank.

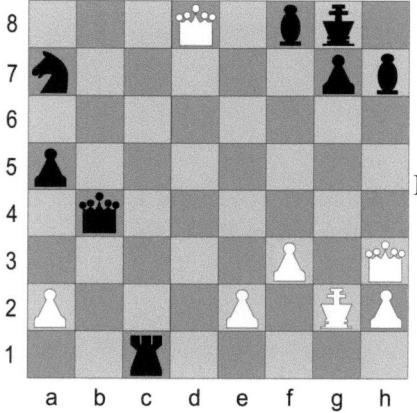

Here, the pawn was promoted to a rook.

Castling – Considered a King's Move

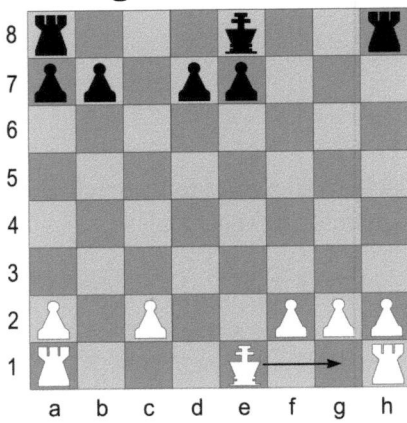

Why would you castle? To get the king to safety, since he's safer in the corner than in the middle of the chessboard.

Castling may only be performed once in a game. There is castling short and castling long. Castling is a move of the king and a rook (of the same color). This is the only move in chess where two pieces are moved and where a king can move two squares.

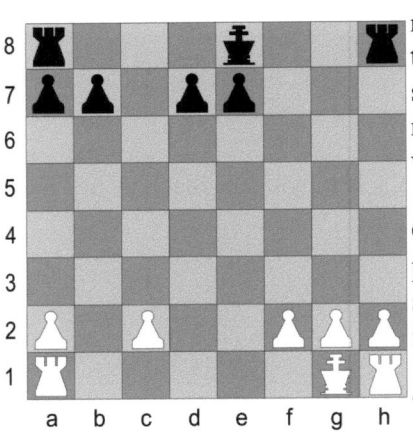

The king (in its initial position) is moved first and moves two squares into the direction of the rook (from the initial square). The rook goes to the square next to the king (jumping over the king), which it just moved over.

Castling short on the white side is performed with the king and rook on square h1. The king moves two squares in the direction of the rook.

The white king moved from square e1 to square g1.

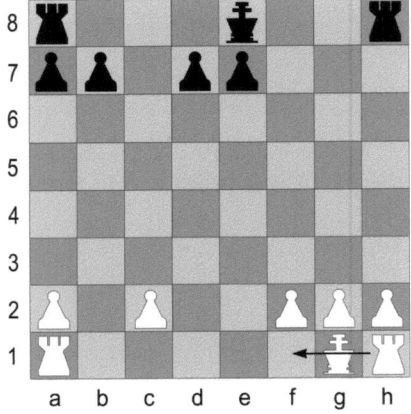

The rook moves (over the king) to the square to the left of the king.

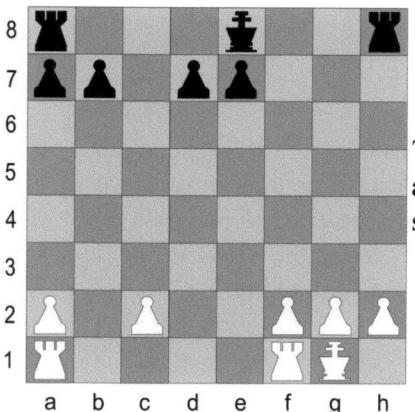

This is what the chessboard looks like after castling short. The king is now on square g1 and the rook is on square f1.

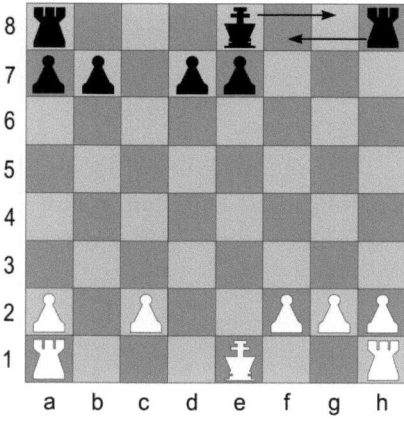

Castling short on the black side is performed with the king and the rook on square h8. The king moves two squares in the direction of the rook. The rook moves (over the king) to the square to the left of the king.

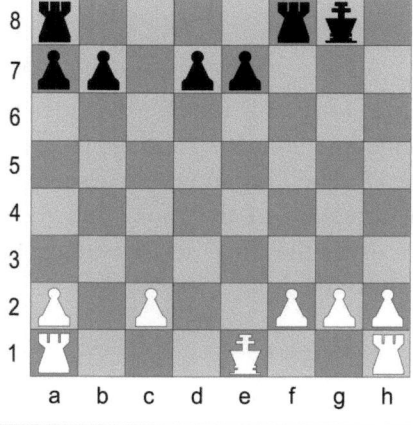

This is what the chessboard looks like after castling short. The king is now on square g8 and the rook is on square f8.

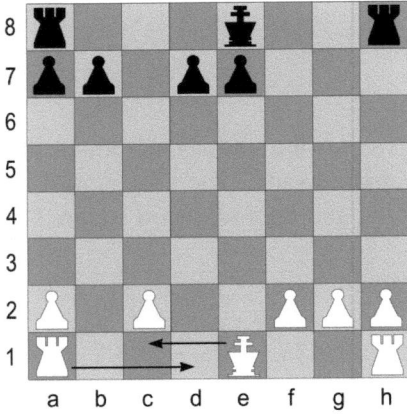

Castling long on the white side is performed with the king and the rook on square a1. The king moves two squares in the direction of the rook. The rook moves (over the king) to the square to the right of the king.

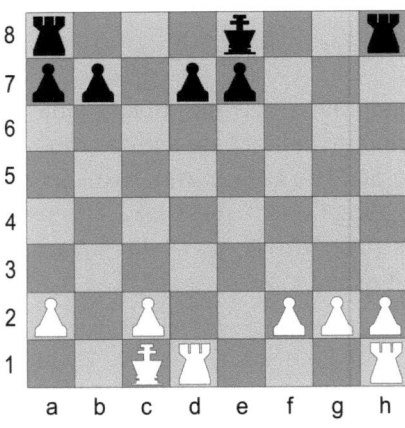

This is what the chessboard looks like after castling long. The king is now on square c1 and the rook is on square d1.

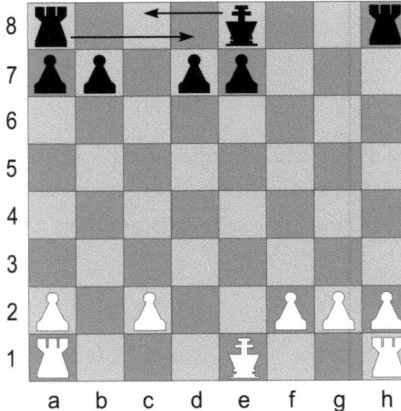

Castling long on the black side is performed with the king and the rook on square a8. The king moves two squares in the direction of the rook. The rook moves (over the king) to the square to the right of the king.

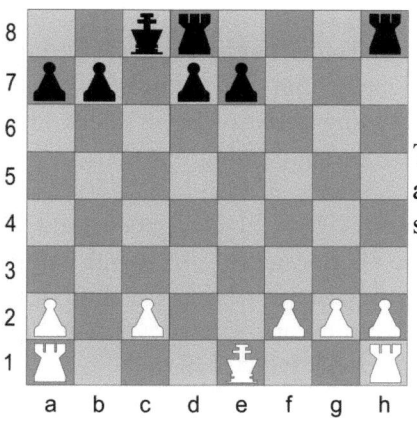

This is what the chessboard looks like after castling long. The king is now on square c8 and the rook is on square d8.

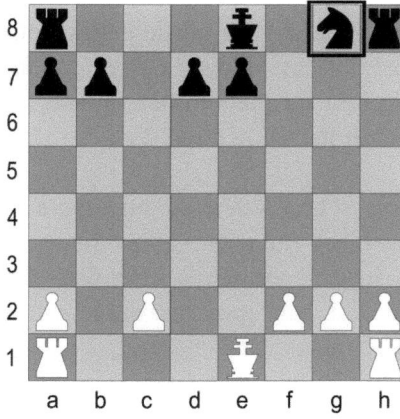

The following rules apply:

1. Between king and rook, there cannot be any of your own or the opponent's pieces.

Example: Black cannot perform castling, because their knight (square g8) is in the way.

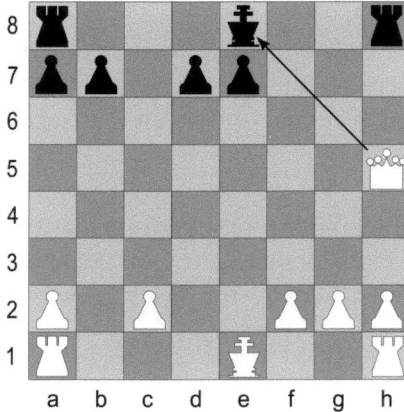

2. The king cannot be in check before castling is performed.

Example: The white queen (square h5) checks the black king (square e8).

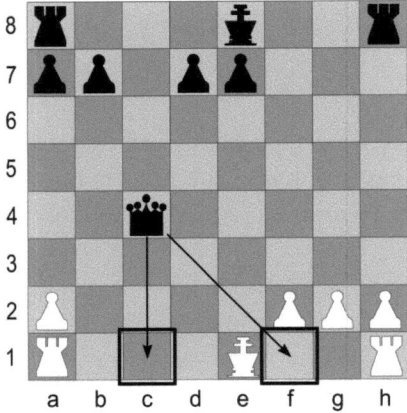

3. The king cannot pass through squares that are attacked by an opposing piece or be in check after performing castling.

Example: The black queen attacks square f1. Because of this, white cannot perform castling short. Castling long also doesn't work, since it would put the king in check (square c1).

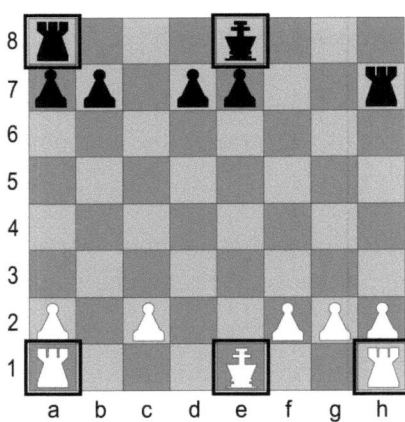

4. The king and the participating rook must not have moved before and are therefore on their initial square, i.e. also on the same rank.

Example: The black rook on square a8 and the black king, as well as the rooks on a1, h1 and the white king were not moved yet and are in their initial position.

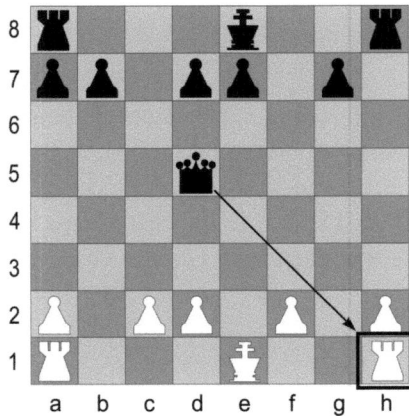

5. The rook is allowed to pass through squares that are attacked or move from its initial square if it is attacked.

Example: White may perform castling short, even though their rook on square h1 is attacked by the black queen on square d5.

Check, Mate, Draw, Stalemate

The object of chess
The object of a game of chess is to "trap" the opponent's king, to "checkmate" it. This is how you win the game.

Check:
When the king is attacked (that is, when an opponent's piece threatens to capture it in the next move), it is in CHECK. This is communicated to the opponent by saying "check". If you do not say this, however, it is not a violation of the rules.

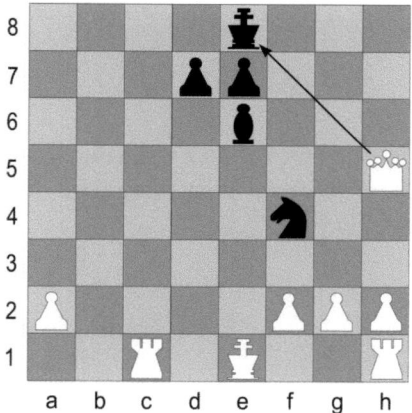

Example: The white queen on square h5 checks the black king on square e8.

Attacks like that have to be repelled in the next move.

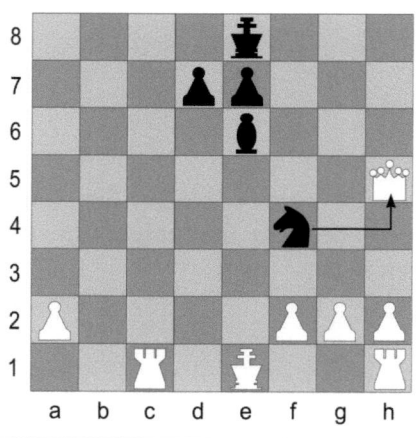

There are three options:

1. Can you capture the checking piece?

The knight moves from square f4 to square h5 and takes the queen.

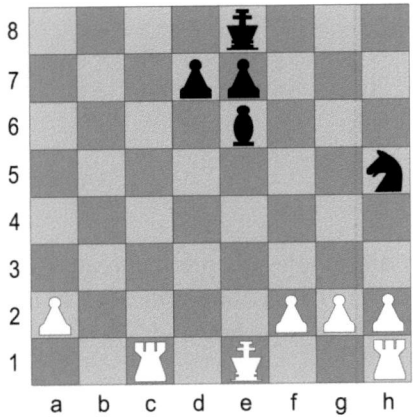

The queen on square h5 was captured.

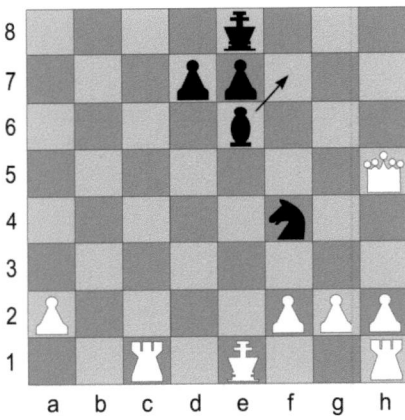

2. Can you move one of your own pieces between your king and the checking piece?

The knight moves from square e6 to square f7.

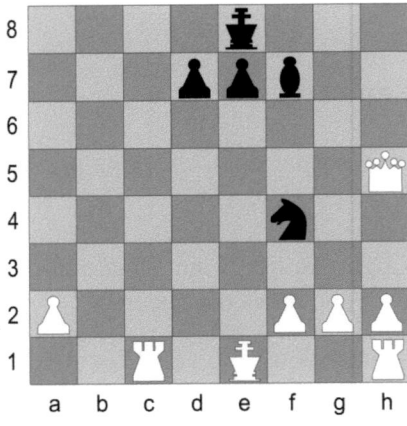

The queen cannot check the king anymore, because the knight moved between them.

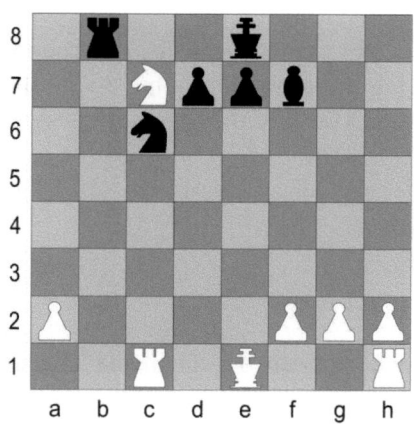

Remember:
If a pawn or knight checks a king, in this case the white knight on square c7, you can move a piece between them.

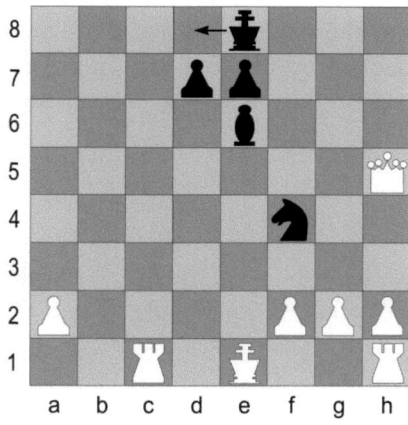

3. Can you move to a square that the king is not attacked on, i.e. move away?

The king moves from square e8 to square d8.

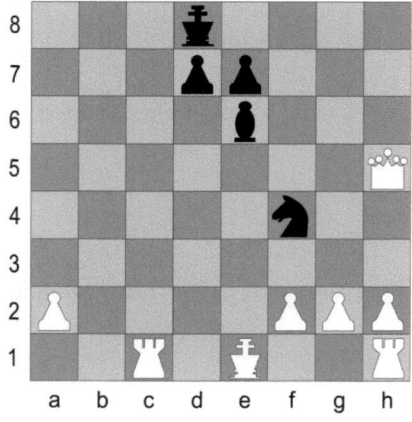

The king was moved out of check.

Mate:

If the king is put into check by one or several opposing pieces and cannot make a move that repels (capturing, moving in-between, moving away) the threat of the opponent's pieces. This is when you lose the game of chess.

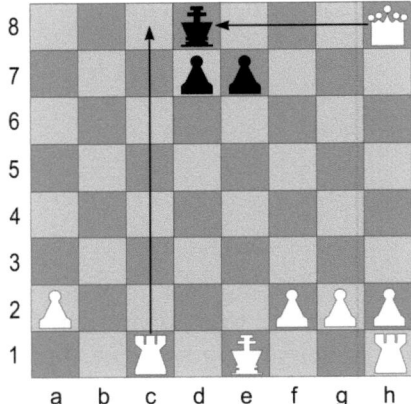

The white queen on square h8 checks the black king on square d8. It cannot move to square e8, because it would still be in check by the queen. It also cannot move to the squares c8 and c7. Those are attacked by the rook on square c1. Because of this, black is checkmated.

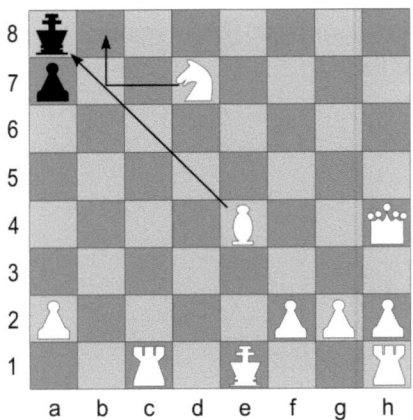

The white bishop on square e4 checks the black king on square a8.

It cannot move to square b7, because it would still be in check by the bishop.

It also cannot move to square b8. It is attacked by the knight.

Because of this, black is checkmated.

Remember:

The king cannot be taken, because the king may not move into being in check.

Draw and Stalemate:

1. If both players see no way of checkmating the opponent or settle on a draw.

2. If both players do not have enough pieces, i.e. a position arises through which no mate can be reached.

3. The last 50 consecutive moves of each player have been made without a pawn being moved or a piece being captured.

4. If the same positioning has occurred for the third time (not necessarily consecutively).

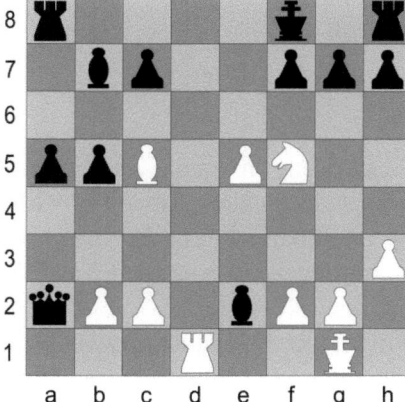

Example: White has less pieces than black and thus, their chance of winning is smaller. Because of this, white makes use of this rule. The white knight moves from square e7 to square f5 and checks with their bishop on square c5. The black king can only move to square g8 (if it moves to square e8, it would be in check in the next move, because the white bishop will move to square g7).

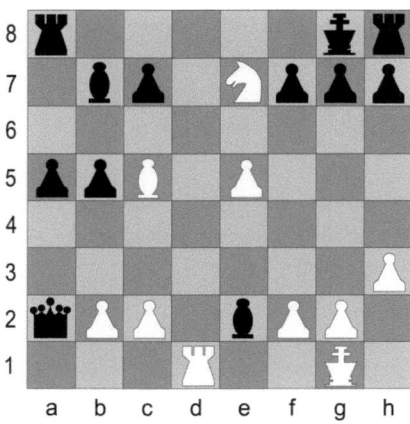

Then, the white bishop moves from square f5 back to square e7 and checks the king again; the king then has to move back to square f8. The same is repeated and the positioning has occurred for the third time.

5. Or through the so-called stalemate. If the king is not in check and can only make moves that check the king and if none of your other pieces can make a move, the game ends in a draw.

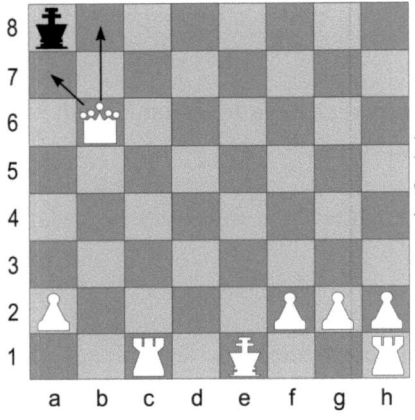

Example: The black king on square a8 can only move into check, because the white queen on square b6 attacks the squares a7, b8 and b7.

The black king on square g8 can only move back into check, since the white bishop on square d6 and the pawn on square h6 attack the squares g7 and f8.

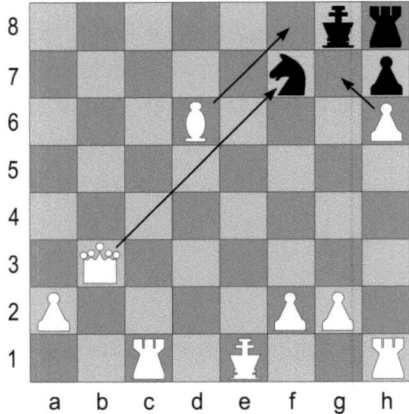

The knight on f7 cannot move away, since this would put the king on square g8 into check.

Furthermore, the black rook on square h8 cannot move because it is blocked by the king on square g8 and the pawn on square h7.

The pawn on square h7 cannot move either, because it is blocked by the pawn on square h6.

Notation of Moves

When notating the moves, the pieces are usually abbreviated with their initial letter.
R = Rook, Kt = Knight, B = Bishop, Q = Queen, K = King.

Pawn moves are noted without the initial letter: a4, c3, e6, b5.

Each move of a piece is noted with the initial and the square it is moving to.
Be5 - d4, Ktf3 - e5, Rd1 - f1, Qd1 - g4.

In the case of a pawn promotion, the initial letter of the new piece it transforms into is mentioned after the pawn's move. a1Q, h1R, d8B, e8Kt.

The moves are numbered. A white move is first, then a black move. It is also mentioned which square the piece came from and where it moves to.

But there is also short notation. In this case, only the squares that the piece moves to is noted.
Bd4, Kte5, Rf1, Qg4 instead of Be5 - d4, Ktf3 - e5, Rd1 - f1, Qd1 - g4.

Example: Detailed notation
1.   e2 – e4   b7 – b6

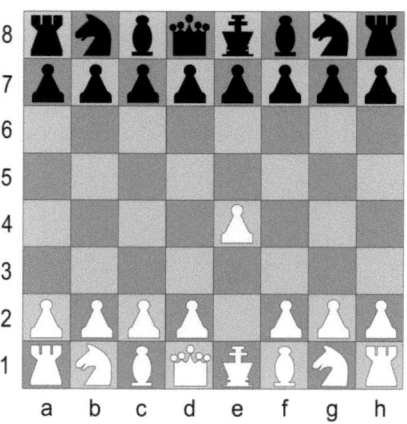 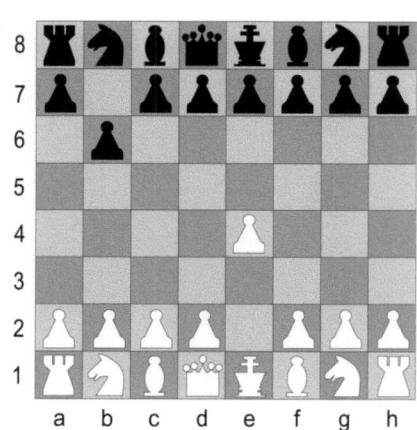

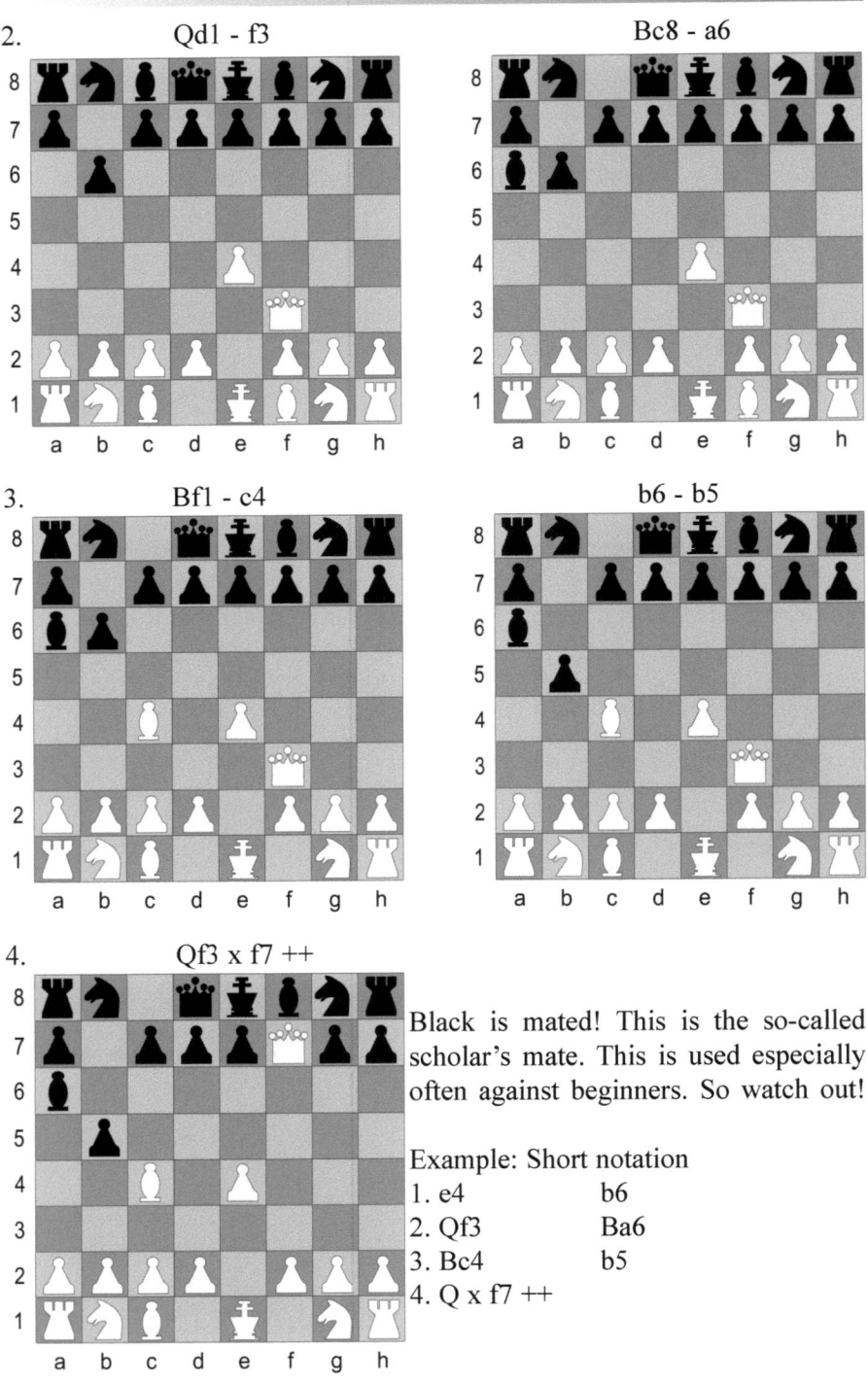

2. Qd1 - f3

Bc8 - a6

3. Bf1 - c4

b6 - b5

4. Qf3 x f7 ++

Black is mated! This is the so-called scholar's mate. This is used especially often against beginners. So watch out!

Example: Short notation
1. e4   b6
2. Qf3   Ba6
3. Bc4   b5
4. Q x f7 ++

Example of a scoresheet:

Tournament: CITY CHAMPIONSHIP			Date: 16.01.2022		
Round: 1			Result: 1:0		
☐ White: FISCHER			■ Black: HACKER		
	White:	Black:		White:	Black:
1	e4	b6	25		
2	Qf3	Bab	26		
3	Bc4	b5	27		
4	Q x F7++		28		
5			29		
6			30		
7			31		
8			32		
9			33		
10			34		
11			35		
12			36		
13			37		
14			38		
15			39		
16			40		
17			41		
18			42		
19			43		
20			44		
21			45		
22			46		
23			47		
24			48		

More Indicators in Notation:

0 - 0	castling short	0 - 0 - 0	castling long
x	indicator for capturing	+	check
=	draw	++ or #	checkmate
e.p.	capture en passant	-	moves from ... to ...
!	good move	?	bad move
1:0	White wins, one point		
0:1	Black wins, one point		
0,5:0,5	Remis, draw, half a point		

The Rules of Chess

1. Before a game of chess, a draw is made to determine who starts with white (white always starts).

2. The two players always make alternating moves.

3. It is compulsory to make a move. When it is your turn, you have to make a move.

4. It is not compulsory to capture. You do not have to capture a piece.

5. Once you touch a piece, you have to make a move with that piece (the touch-move rule). If this is not possible, there are no consequences.

6. If you touch one of your opponent's pieces, you have to capture it. If this is not possible, there are no consequences.

7. If you want to adjust a piece, you have to say "I adjust" first.

8. The king has to be removed from any check. If this is overlooked, the moves that were made afterwards have to be reversed.

9. A move that doesn't comply with the rules of chess has to be reversed.

Small Exercises

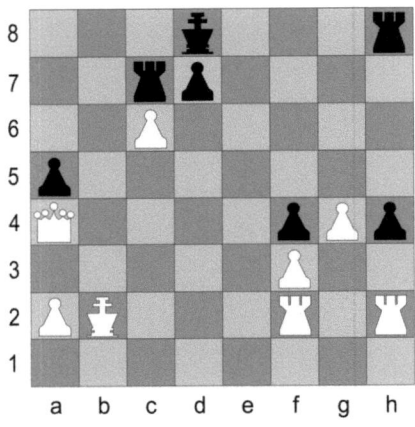

Exercise 1:
White moves from square g2 to square g4. It is black's turn. What is a very good move black can make now?

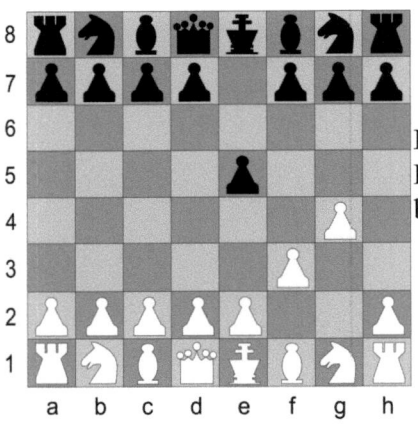

Exercise 2:
It is black's turn. Which move should black make now?

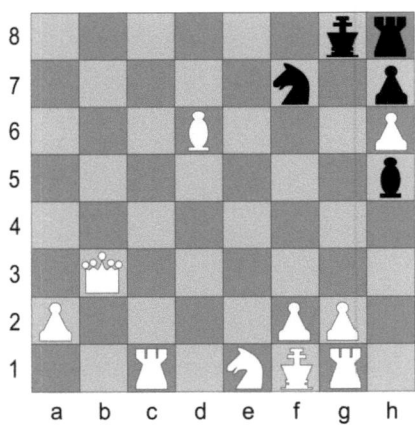

Exercise 3:
It is black's turn. Which move should black make now?

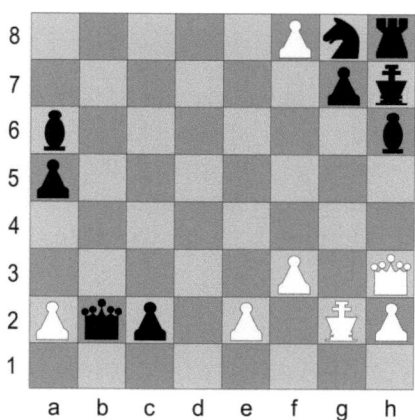

Exercise 4:
White moves to square f8. What piece should white exchange for their pawn?

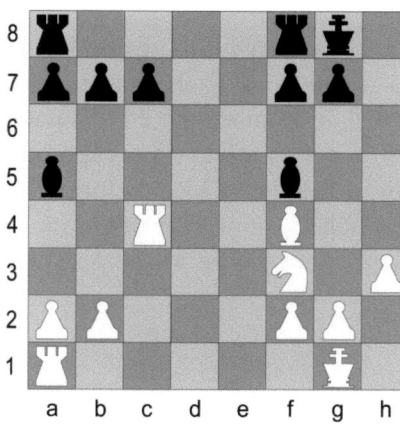

Exercise 5:
It is white's turn. Which move should white make now?

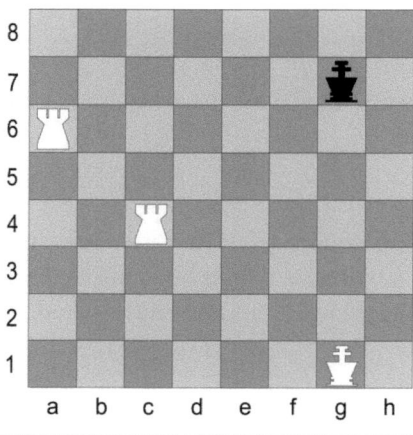

Exercise 6:
It is white's turn. Which move should white make now to checkmate black?

If you have solved the exercises correctly, you have mastered the basic rules.

Answers are on the next page.

Answers:

Exercise 1:
Capturing en passant (in passing). Since the white pawn has moved forward two squares from its initial position on square g2 to square g4. This way, the black pawn (square f4) can move to square g3 and capture the white pawn on square g4. And for the next move, black can also capture a rook. Don't move the pawn on h4, because the white rook on h2 will take the black rook on h8.

Exercise 2:
Black moves their queen to square h4 and checkmates white. White has played as badly as possible. This is the quickest checkmate.

Exercise 3:
Black has fewer pieces than white and the position also works against black. In the next move, black would be mated (white rook from square c1 to square c8). That's why black moves their bishop from square h5 to square e2 and checks the white king. All that's left for the king to do is capturing the bishop and it moves to square e2. Now it would be black's turn. The black king on square g8 can only move into check now. The knight on f7 cannot move away, since the king on square g8 would be in check. Thus, black has achieved a stalemate.

Exercise 4:
Promotion to a bishop. This way, the black king is in check. Since the king cannot move to square g6, which is threatened by the knight and black cannot capture the knight, black is checkmated.

Exercise 5:
Moving the rook from square c4 to square c5. This way, the white rook can take one of the bishops in their next move.

Exercise 6:
White moves their rook from square c4 to square c7. The king can only move to a square in the 8th rank. White's next move would be to move their rook from square a6 to square a8. This way, black would be checkmated.

Tips for Your First Game of Chess

Congratulations! You now know the rules of chess.

You might think, let's get right to playing! But not so fast. Without further knowledge, you will quickly lose, at least the first few games, and possibly think that chess is not for you after all. Therefore, here are a few tips.

1. Write down your games. This way you can analyze your mistakes later.

2. Occupy the center:
This would be the squares d4, e4, e5 and d5.

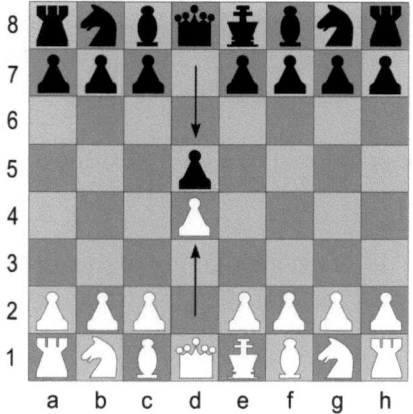

White opens with d4 (black opens with d7 – d5) or …

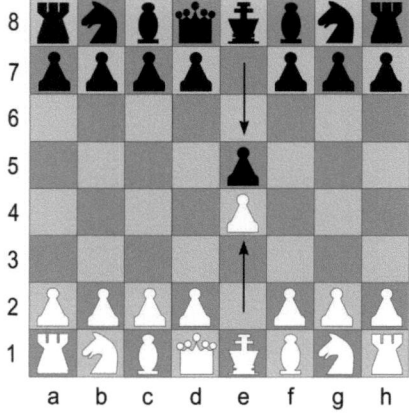

… with e4. Black then opens with the double move of the opposite pawn, e7 – e5.

This also opens up the possibility to develop your bishop.

Tips for Your First Game of Chess

3. Developing pieces:

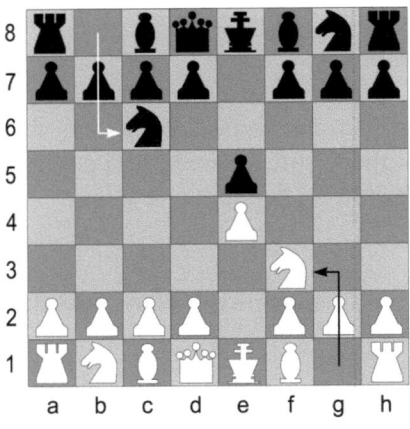

Develop your minor pieces (bishop, knight) right at the start. This also helps with occupying the center.

White develops their knight and at the same time attacks the black pawn on square e5.

Black also develops their black knight and reacts to the threat of the white knight. They protect their pawn on e5.

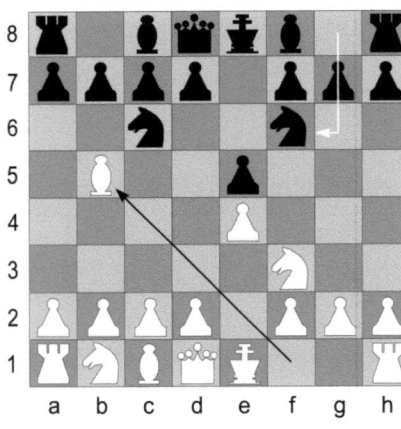

The white bishop is developed and attacks the black knight on square c6.

White could castle in their next move.

Black develops their knight to square f6. With this, they threaten the white pawn on square e4.

4. Castling as early as possible:

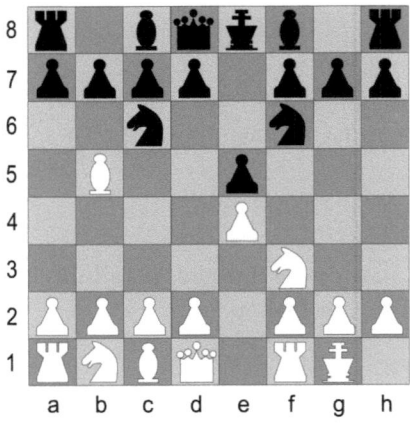

White castles and thus puts their king in a safe position.

5. Protect your pieces:
   Covering material (pieces) / attacking material

Material is the term used to describe the pieces in chess. We have already learned what the value of each piece is.

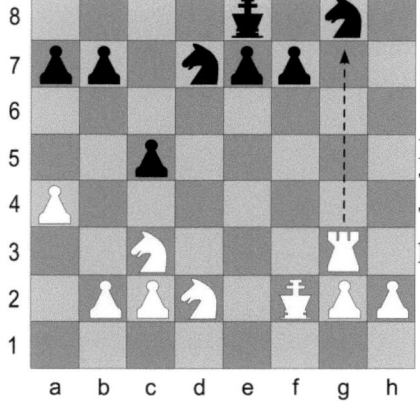

Example:
The rook on g3 attacks the knight on g8. The white rook could take the black knight in the next move.

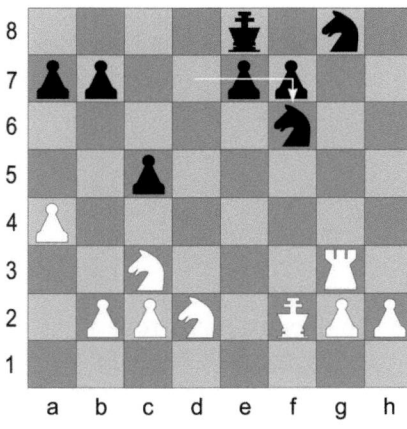

But now the black knight moves from square d7 to square f6 and covers the knight that is being attacked. The material was covered, so the opponent could not capture the piece.

6. Winning material / losing material

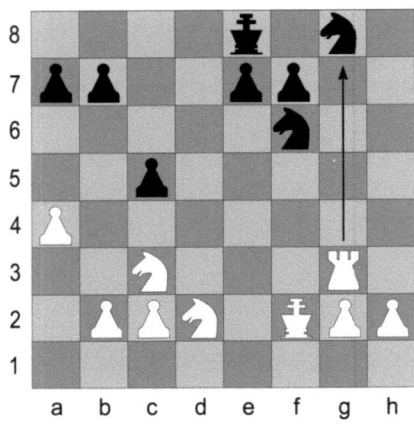

It is important for someone learning chess not to lose material. That means to keep your pieces.

An example:
The white rook on square g3 moves to square g8 …

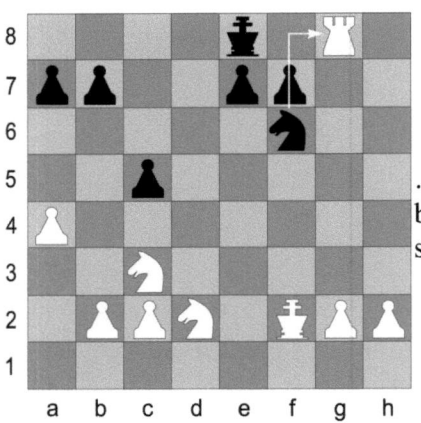

… and takes the black knight. The other black knight on square f6 now moves to square g8 …

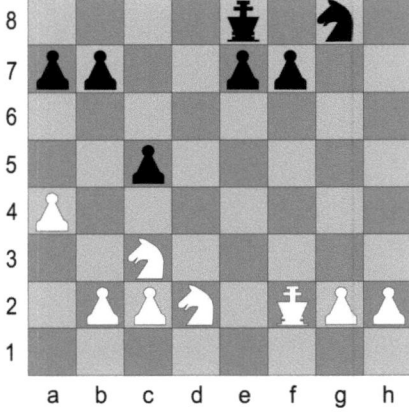

… and captures the white rook.

If you lose your rook and capture a knight, theoretically, your opponent would have two more pawns on the chessboard. This is called a loss of material for us and a gain of material for the opponent.

And the difference between a major and a minor piece is also called exchange. In this case, we have lost exchange.

7. Sacrifices

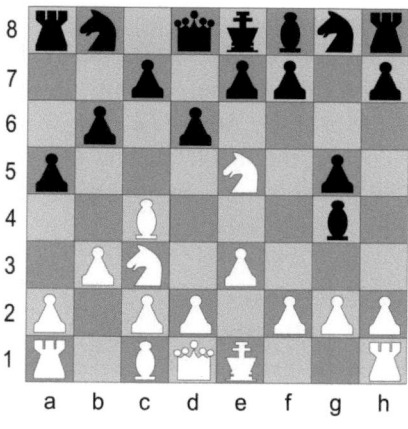

Intentionally allowing your opponent to capture one of your pieces. In doing this, you hope for an advantage.

In this example, white gives up their queen to be captured. White has moved their knight from square f3 to square e5. Black now captures the queen on d1 with the bishop on g4. This was a mistake. The bishop moves from square c4 to f7 and black is mated.

8. Fork

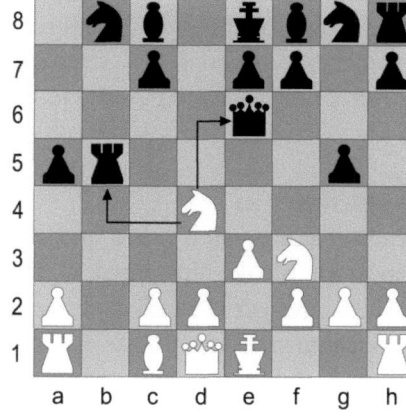

If a piece attacks two of the opponent's pieces at the same time.

The white knight on square d4 threatens the black queen on square e6 and the black rook on square b5.

Black can now save either the queen on the rook. One of the pieces is lost.

9. Zugzwang ("compulsion to move")

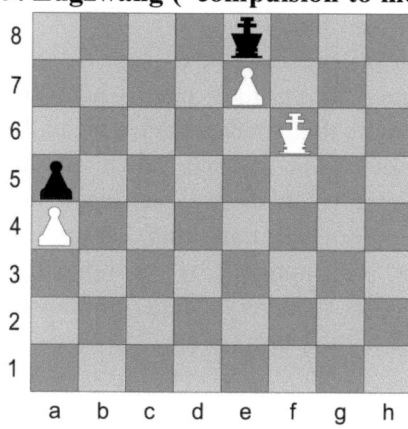

If you have to make a move but don't want to.

The black king has to make a move and loses the game because of this.

1. e7   Kd7
2. Kf7   Kc7
3. e8Q

10. The pawn positions

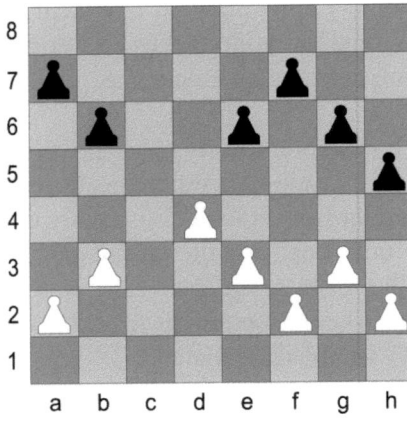

The pawn chain

Occupying/controlling the center with your pawns during the opening. If the pawns cover each other, i.e. the front pawn covers the back pawn, this is called a pawn chain. In a chain, the pawns have great security.

The isolated pawn

In the middlegame, usually only isolated pawn chains are formed or they are scattered individually.

In chess, an isolated pawn is a pawn that can no longer cover the other pawns. They are weak and easily captured. They must be covered by stronger pieces. Here, those are the pawns on d6, d3 and f7.

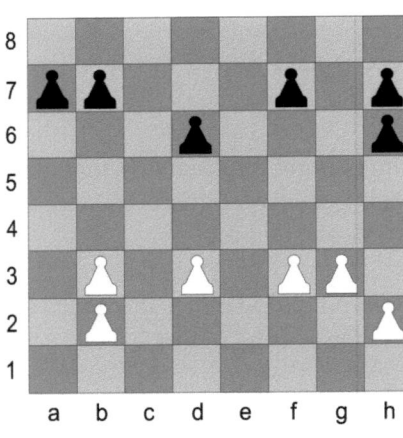

The doubled pawns

They cannot cover each other and the pawn in front blocks the pawn in the back. They are very weak and even easier to capture. Here, those are the pawns on b2 and b3, as well as h7 and h6.

The passed pawn

The less pieces there are in the endgame, the stronger pawns become. To promote them makes them especially dangerous. The passed pawn is the pawn that is on its way to reach the opponent's back rank and cannot be blocked or captured by an opposing pawn. This is a very dangerous pawn. Here, it is the pawn on d3.

11. Gaining a tempo

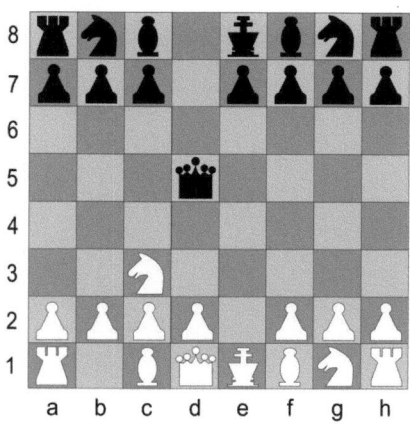

A move to develop your pieces more quickly than your opponent.

White moves their bishop from square b1 to square c3. By doing this, white attacks the black queen. Black has to move the queen away, so white as gained a tempo.

12. Losing a tempo

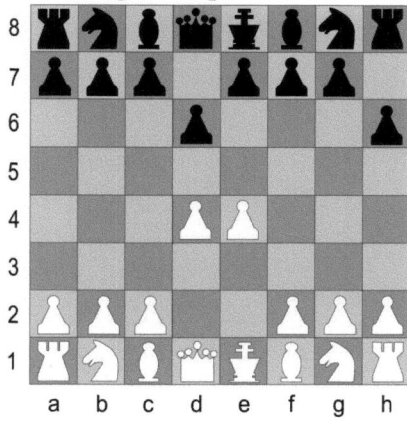

A move that does not contribute to the development or improvement of the position of your pieces.

The move of the black pawn from square h7 to square h6 doesn't do anything. Because of this, we speak of losing a tempo here.

13. Develop your pieces so that they cannot be chased away by your opponent's pieces.

14. The queen should not be moved too early. If it is, it is best to move it to e2 or e7.

15. Don't move the knight to the edge.

16. Don't think just one, but multiple moves ahead. That includes your opponent's moves. So: Always think before making a move!

I hope you have a lot of fun and success playing chess!